# Investment Project Controlling with SAP®

Michael Esser

# Thank you for purchasing this book from Espresso Tutorials!

Like a cup of espresso coffee, Espresso Tutorials SAP books are concise and effective. We know that your time is valuable and we deliver information in a succinct and straightforward manner. It only takes our readers a short amount of time to consume SAP concepts. Our books are well recognized in the industry for leveraging tutorial-style instruction and videos to show you step by step how to successfully work with SAP.

Check out our YouTube channel to watch our videos at
*https://www.youtube.com/user/EspressoTutorials*.

If you are interested in SAP Finance and Controlling, join us at
*http://www.fico-forum.com/forum2/*
to get your SAP questions answered and contribute to discussions.

## Related titles from Espresso Tutorials:

- ▶ Martin Munzel: New SAP® Controlling Planning Interface
  *http://5011.espresso-tutorials.com*
- ▶ Dieter Schlagenhauf & Jörg Siebert: SAP® Fixed Assets Accounting (FI-AA)
  *http://5023.espresso-tutorials.com*
- ▶ Anurag Barua: First Steps in the SAP® Crystal Reports
  *http://5017.espresso-tutorials.com*
- ▶ Stefan Eifler: Quick Guide to SAP® CO-PA (Profitability Analysis)
  *http://5018.espresso-tutorials.com*
- ▶ Kermit Bravo & Scott Cairncross: SAP® Enterprise Performance Management (EP;) Add-In
  *http://5042.espresso-tutorials.com*
- ▶ Tanya Duncan: Practical Guide to SAP® CO-PC (Product Cost Controlling)
  *http://5064.espresso-tutorials.com*
- ▶ Ann Cacciottolli: First Steps in SAP® Financial Accounting (FI)
  *http://5095.espresso-tutorials.com*

Michael Esser
**Investment Project Controlling with SAP®**

**ISBN:**         978-1-51728386-5

**Editor:**       Alice Adams

**Cover Design:**   Philip Esch, Martin Munzel

**Cover Photo:**   Fotolia: #43451195 © Maxim_Kazmin

**Feedback**
We greatly appreciate any kind of feedback you have concerning this book. Please mail us at *info@espresso-tutorials.com*.

# Table of Contents

# Preface

This book is about investment controlling with a special focus on development projects, which means that a new asset is built as a result of the project. We will also discuss variations of development projects, like turnaround or major overhauls, as well as Joint Venture projects. We'll start with a high level, strategic view and then drilldown into the details of how to use the individual applications in SAP-PS.

This book will primarily be of interest to project controllers, in addition to any project-focused professionals in charge of holding or requesting project funds. Furthermore, it will also be useful for individuals from contracting and procurement disciplines as it covers the complete process from the planning, purchasing, construction, and reporting points of view. My personal recommendation is to read the book from the beginning to end in order to understand the big picture before diving into the details.

Tips highlight information concerning more details about the subject being described and/or additional background information.

 Examples help illustrate a topic better by relating it to real world scenarios.

 Warnings draw attention to information that you should be aware of when you go through the examples from this book on your own.

Finally, a note concerning the copyright: All screenshots printed in this book are the copyright of SAP SE. All rights are reserved by SAP SE. Copyright pertains to all SAP images in this publication. For simplification, we will not mention this specifically underneath every screenshot.

# 1 Introduction

*"Midway upon the journey of our life I found myself within a forest dark, For the straightforward pathway had been lost."*

*DANTE ALIGHIERI, The Divine Comedy*

This book offers practical advice – written by a practitioner for practitioners. My inspiration was on one hand my current job as project finance manager/ project controller, and on the other, my vision of project management as the most frequent working method of the 21$^{st}$ century. In branches like plant engineering and construction, working in interdisciplinary project teams is already a common part of the existing working culture. In large organizations, projects are an integrated part of day-to-day business. Increasingly, medium sized entities are also integrating projects in to their work practices. This is underpinned by technologies, which enable working together in virtual and very flexible organizations spread around the globe, no longer requiring permanent physical presence.

This book includes my personal experiences as a project controller in the oil industry, as well as my recommendations on how to set up a seamless controlling project in SAP-PS, that I think are worth sharing with a broader audience working with SAP-PS. In this book, I'll not only make recommendations related to SAP, but also other subjects from my professional practice. In particular, I want to share both my best practices of how to use SAP-PS as a controlling tool within major projects, as well as controlling best practices, e.g. a permanent tracking of commitments or stakeholder management. Although I have gained my personal experiences from the oil industry, these recommendations are relevant for controlling teams working with investment controlling functionality in a variety of industries.

I have kept the theoretical part of each chapter to a minimum and have included screenshots and process flows in order to make the relevant topics visible and applicable. At the end of the book, I will provide several practical tips and tricks from my own experience working on large Brownfield projects in the oil industry.

**Brownfield & Greenfield projects**

 Brownfield is a technical term used in the oil industry for projects that are executed in an existing venue, e.g. a refinery or a chemical plant. A Greenfield development project means that a completely new asset is built.

I have selected four basic project processes that will form the foundation of each chapter. The phases are: planning, design, execution, and completion. We will focus on SAP activities in each separate phase. In fact, there may be several additional phases depending on the industry or branch in which the project is carried out. But for the purposes of this book, the project process is set up as an archetype with well known designations.

Let's take a look at how this e-book is structured and what will be covered in each chapter. In Chapter 1 I will provide foundational information, e.g. the modules used in SAP for planning and controlling purposes and how they are linked to one another. Moreover, you will learn which kind of projects exist, like development projects, where something completely new is built or turnaround projects, which cover major overhauls on existing assets. Also an important part of the introductory chapter will be an understanding of funding including which funds can be requested and what kind of budgetary controls are used within budget controlling. I will also provide further explanation on how a project structure can be put into SAP-PS and how SAP numbers the projects consecutively.

The introductory chapter ends with a brief overview of the project process. The project process will provide a framework for the entire book.

In Chapter 2 I will introduce individual roles and responsibilities working in projects and their specific roles. For example, there are individuals who hold funds or set up project structures in SAP, or are responsible for reporting of single projects or project portfolios.

The Chapter 3 covers the aforementioned project process with special regard to the single project phases. Theses phases are:

- ▶ Planning
- ▶ Design
- ▶ Execution
- ▶ Completion

The activities in SAP differ from phase to phase, but nevertheless it is important to mention the impact of each phase on the project success in general.

The separate project scenarios are covered in Chapter 4. The master type of project, if not mentioned otherwise, is that of a Greenfield development project. That means that a completely new asset is built. But there is always the possibility of carrying out a revamp or a rejuvenation of already existing assets, which includes major overhaul projects. These major overhauls are known within the oil and gas industry, as well as in the chemical industry as turnaround projects. As these types of projects contain the renewal or exchange of huge amounts of smaller equipment, they also require a certain kind of handling, e.g. for purchasing purposes. So in addition to the networks and network activities, which are also used in development projects, I will introduce the concept of maintenance work orders. These orders are used similarly to network activities. Network activities and all other available project symbols are illustrated in Figure 1.7.

Projects in the oil industry require large investments that are often executed jointly by two or more companies. The archetype is a joint venture project, which is also introduced in Chapter 4. The most common form of a joint venture contains two parties and is carried out for a certain period of time. Joint ventures can either be entity led, led by a third party, or joint venture partner. So I will introduce both the project profile in SAP and the process.

Chapter 5 contains a summary overview of the available reports in SAP in order to track project costs. Moreover the most common report in the oil industry, the OC1-sheet, is introduced. OC1 is an abbreviation for overall costs, which indicates that this report contains all costs for a certain project number within SAP.

Chapter 6 contains my personal recommendations for setting up a smooth controlling project, including mostly my personal experiences gained in the oil industry. Last but not least, I will provide a section containing definitions and acronyms used throughout the book.

So I have chosen to approach this book starting with general information and moving to more detailed and very specific information, because I think this suits the usability of this book for readers who are not part of the oil industry. From my personal experience as controller, I am aware of other industries that use SAP-PS in a very similar way as I have described in book including telecommunications, real estate and logistics.

**Industries that use SAP-PS**

 In addition to the oil industry, there are several other industries that use SAP-PS similarly including the telecommunications, real estate, and logistics industries.

Furthermore, chapter four about project concepts focuses on the roles and responsibilities of a project controller. The setup of a commercial department within the project will also be introduced briefly, as it is key to embed the controlling function with the other commercial disciplines like contracting and procurement, scheduling, cost engineering and risk management. Usually there are three rather similar teams/departments in the project. The first one is dependent on the size of the project, the finance team. This team deals with traditional finance topics like reporting, accounting and invoice management. The other team is the project services team, which covers cost engineering, scheduling and risk management. The third team is the contracting and procurement team, which has also an important role in claims management.

## 1.1 SAP Modules "Landscape"

This chapter will cover a brief overview of the SAP modules covering investment planning and controlling topics and how they are linked together, in other words the "system landscape". Moreover, the IM structure and funding will be discussed briefly.

Figure 1.1: SAP modules shows the SAP modules, or the landscape. SEM-BPS contains the high level planning, ranking, and reporting per Class of Business. Investment Management (IM) comprises the release and allocation of capital funds to individual projects, reflecting functional approval. The execution, as well as the detailed planning, is carried out in the Project Systems Module (PS). As stated above, this e-book deals mainly with execution in the PS module.

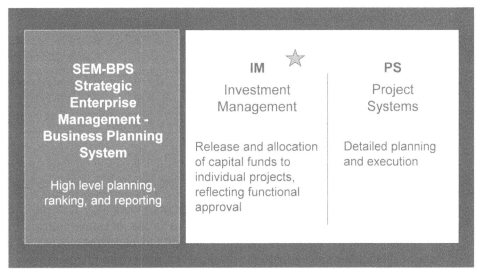

*Figure 1.1: SAP modules*

## 1.2 IM Structure

The following is an example (see Figure 1.2) from the retail business and demonstrates the IM module structure. I would like to give you some additional details about how the IM module is structured. On the top level is always the class of business (COB), e.g. Retail. Then this COB line can be drilled down further to the next level, which is what the general manager is responsible for in terms of COB and network planning. This indicates a more strategic point of view. The next level shows the development plan separated in to regions or countries. Thereafter, the plan manager for region or country is available. The last drill down line contains the new market entries.

Primarily, I will focus on SAP-PS where projects are carried out.

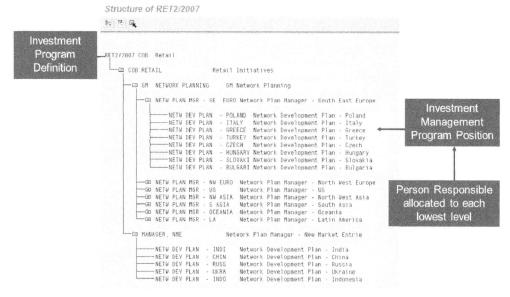

*Figure 1.2: IM structure, example from the retail business*

The highest level applicable is the investment program definition. It is set up only on class of business level. The next level is the investment program position, with the person responsible allocated to each lowest level. This is a rather pragmatic approach, because the authorities should not be allocated to senior executives only. The system also accepts delegates, if the responsible person is unavailable.

## 1.3 CAPEX funds

The most common term for investment funds or investment money in the oil and gas industry is CAPEX, which means capitalized expenditures. In the entities reporting this indicates assets shown in the balance sheet, mostly under the section property, plant and equipment (PPE). However, from an accounting point of view not all expenditures can be capitalized. These expenditures are called REVEX. This is a technical term for revenue expenditures, which means that the costs defined as REVEX are shown in the profit and loss account, mostly in the section other entity related costs, e.g. cleaning or demolishing works.

## CAPEX and REVEX

The most common term for investment funds or in-vestment money in the oil and gas industry is CAPEX, which means capitalized expenditures. Expenditures that cannot be capitalized are called REVEX. This is a technical term for revenue expend-itures, which means that the costs defined as REVEX are shown in the profit and loss account.

| Funds Allocated in USD | | Availability Control in Local Currency |
|---|---|---|
| $130 USD allocated | Exchange Rate 1,3 : 1 | = €100 to spend |

No currency fluctuation in available funds caused by exchange rate

*Figure 1.3: CAPEX funds*

When a different exchange rate is used in the investment proposal from the annual budget planning rate, you must recognize the currency impact when entering budgets into SAP and requesting release of funds. CAPEX Funds are requested in USD and translated into local currency at the annual budget planning rate. CAPEX is an abbreviation for capital-ized expenditures, which means, that the settlement of actuals has an impact on the balance sheet, within the section of property, plant and equipment (PPE).

The budget control in the PS module operates in local currency (€). The IM module operates in USD. There is one fixed exchange rate per year based on the annual planning rate available. In the event that a major currency fluctuation in the available funds hampers the course of the project, the initiation of a supplemental investment proposal is allowed. Hence the project should be able to spend the funds originally approved for final investment decision. The CAPEX fund request is processed via workflow within the portal, a web based application, which is also used for login purposes.

## 1.4 Budgetary Controls

The controls carried out within SAP PS are comparable to those of a traffic light system. Table 1.1 demonstrates how the controls are applied:

| Budget Allocated | Traffic Light | Consequences |
|---|---|---|
| < 80% | Green | - |
| 80% | Yellow | Warning sign occurs |
| 105% | Red | Project is blocked |

*Table 1.1: Budget controls*

Budget allocation figures contained the actuals already posted on the account assignments, as well as the commitments made for contracts and purchase orders. The total commitments also include purchase requisitions, which also block funds.

Once the budget exceeds 105%, the project is completely blocked. No further transactions can be carried out, for example purchase requisitions. In special cases, the release of the blocked project requires a request to the system administrator.

## 1.5 Types of Projects

There are at least eight different types of tax-specific projects that can be set up in SAP. I will explain each of these projects briefly in a subsequent chapter. These project types often differ according to industry and accounting requirements.

We'll cover the following types of projects:

- ▶ Development projects
- ▶ Joint venture projects
- ▶ Turnaround projects

We'll also cover the abandonment of projects.

Development projects are the standard project profile for the majority of construction (and demolition) projects. For CAPEX projects, you will create assets under construction. Assets under construction (AuC) is an interim account in the balance sheet that will be used prior to the capitalization and final settlement of the project. Another well known term used in place of AuC is work in progress (WiP). Further work is required to ensure an object is ready to use. REVEX WBS elements are **not statistical**! REVEX is an abbreviation for revenue expenditure, and indicates that the settlement of expenses has an impact on the profit and loss account. Statistical elements are set up in order to collect costs. Their settlement has neither an impact on the balance sheet, nor on the profit and loss account. These elements are used for internal cost allocation purposes only and their settlement is received from cost centers only. REVEX elements usually include the civil and demolition work carried out in a Brownfield Project. The expenditure related to these types of work is settled within the profit and loss account.

Statistical elements are not visible within the standard report used to track large investment projects. This report is the so-called OC1-sheet; OC1 is an abbreviation for overall costs thus all project related cost should be included in this report. I will cover additional information related this report in section 5.2.

Joint venture projects are often used within the oil and gas industry and are a commonly accepted practice. A joint venture is defined as a contractual agreement whereby two or more parties undertake an economic activity that is subject to joint control. Joint control is the contractually agreed sharing of control of an economic activity. Joint ventures are directly linked to large investments and in allocating the miscellaneous risks in project execution. The archetype of a Joint Venture consists of a 50:50 share split with regards to the funding, as well as to the board members. Moreover, these kind of organizations are set up temporarily, e.g. for the duration of five years. So joint ventures are chosen in order to minimize the financial burden.

Turnaround projects are also a commonly accepted practice, well known in petro-chemical ventures. Turnaround is another term for an inspection that is carried out on a regular basis. Because of its large parameters, it is carried out as project. The turnaround cycle, usually five years, is defined in legislative guidelines. Prior to the setup as investment projects, TA's were executed as large maintenance projects. But due to a major change in accounting practices, i.e. the change in the IAS 16 in early 2005, it is now mandatory to set up a Turnaround Project as an Investment Project. Prior to this, turnaround projects were settled via the profit and loss account. Since 2005 they are settled via the balance sheet. An asset has to be created and depreciated using the straightforward method and the turnaround cycle is usually 5 years.

Statistical projects are primarily used for internal cost allocation. They are not assigned to WBS elements but to work orders which settle their costs to a G/L-account combined with a cost center. Work orders are used to track maintenance costs only. Alternatively these projects are used to track internal process costs. These projects deal with a large number of transactions covering small amounts of revenue with low risk work orders and are more pragmatic to use than WBS elements.

Direct asset purchase / intangible investment projects allow the purchase of "finished" or "ready" assets. The project structure must be used to get access to CAPEX and use **statistical** WBS elements. A typical example for a direct asset purchase is buying a new truck for the fire department. After delivery of the truck, the project can finally be settled as an asset into the balance sheet. This type of projects consists of WBS elements only and does not use network activities.

Cost recovery projects replace internal orders and should be used for all non-ongoing cases where costs should be on-charged or recovered. These types of projects are either intra group projects or in use to allocate costs to 3$^{rd}$ parties, but they are never investment projects.

Process cost reporting (statistical) enables more detailed reporting of costs within cost centers. The number of cost centers and cost elements in SAP are more restricted and statistical projects allow further analysis, e.g. to analyze types of marketing spend.

Asset retirement obligation is used to support assets / provisions required for future financial obligations to clean up sites, etc. This type of project is often used within upstream business or within the mining industry. These obligations are based upon the legal obligation that arises as a result of the acquisition, construction, or development of a long-lived asset. Upstream projects are mostly offshore drilling platforms. After a period of e.g. thirty years the platform has to be decommissioned and demolished. The place where the project was carried out has, due to legislation guidelines, to be left in the statue it was in at the beginning of the project. The obligation is an accounting requirement (liability), which contains the amount of money necessary to rebuild or demolish the asset used for the project, e.g. a platform, a well or a drilling rig.

## 1.6   Project Builder

This section will look at the basic structures within a project module, the work breakdown structure (WBS), network activities and milestones. I will explain each of these elements in detail. I will then follow with an explanation of how to use these elements in SAP.

First, a work breakdown structure is used to cluster a project due to its scope in order to track and plan costs, revenues, and due dates. In the PS module a work breakdown structure needs a project definition upfront, which assigns a unique number for the project and includes some default settings, e.g. the organizational units, currencies, steering parameters, etc. In addition to the project definition, the work breakdown structure contains work breakdown structure (WBS) elements.

These WBS elements can, for example, be equal to the project phases, e.g. planning, design, execution, and completion. I recommend setting up a single element for each work package. An analogy to this structure is clustering the following organizational units as follows. First, there should be WBS elements for the employees of the entity, second for affiliate staff and third, for contracted staff, e.g. for the EPCM-partners. The Project Builder is a standard application (transactional code CJ20N) used to create a WBS structure for the aforementioned types of projects. You can see the Project Builder with a project hierarchy in Figure 1.4.

The project hierarchy can be used for navigational purposes within the project. The degree of granulation displayed can be adjusted in the default settings for the display mode. We will cover project hierarchy and display mode settings in more detail in Chapter 3.2 on Planning Phases.

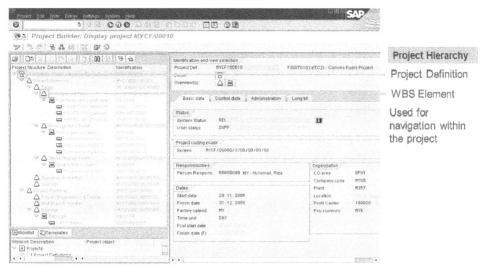

*Figure 1.4: Project hierarchy*

The work list (see Figure 1.5) contains different project templates and current projects. The elements available can easily be moved and inserted into the hierarchy using drag and drop functionality. If one element becomes obsolete it can also be deleted. However, if you delete an element you must ensure that there are no actuals settled or accruals posted. In this case, the settlement for the entire period end has to be reversed!

*Figure 1.5: Work list*

Within the Project Builder, all information for the selected node is displayed in the hierarchy panel (see Figure 1.6).

Project Detail

Displays information for the selected node in the hierarchy panel

Figure 1.6: Project detail

Project Symbols

Project Definition

WBS Element

Network Header

Network Activity

Figure 1.7: Available project symbols

All project symbols necessary to create a WBS structure are available. These are project definitions, WBS elements, network headers, and network activities. These can be moved via drag and drop from the work list to the navigation panel.

## 1.7 Project Numbering Convention

In this section, we will familiarize ourselves with the project numbering convention, which is shown in Figure 1.9, an alphanumeric code explicitly dedicated to one project / project definition. Due to the various types of projects, there are different types of codes that always start with the country code and the business unit where the project is executed. Each project code is unique, in order to identify projects directly from their coding.

The coding also indicates the various project phases and allows for proper cost monitoring for each phase, for each sub-project, and for the complete project structure. Figure 1.8 and Figure 1.9 illustrate the numbering convention for different types of projects.

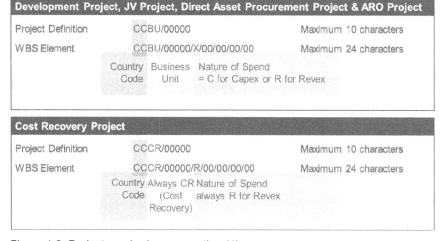

*Figure 1.8: Project numbering convention (1)*

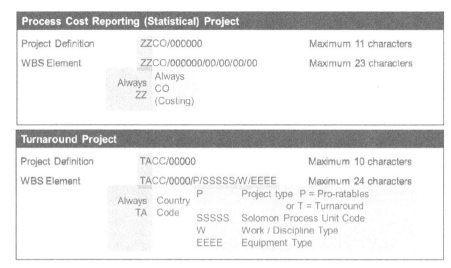

*Figure 1.9: Project numbering convention (2)*

## 1.8 Project Process Overview

The basic project process overview (see Figure 1.10) will serve as guidance during this entire book. Controlling activities and transaction codes in SAP are presented in each section. SAP activities and their relevant transaction codes are listed below each pillar symbolizing one separate project phase.

In the planning phase, the WBS structure is typically designed and created within the 'Project Builder' (transaction code CJ20N). Moreover, the WBS elements are linked to the IM structure, in order to have the investment ('CAPEX') funds available. After building the structure the WBS elements must be released.

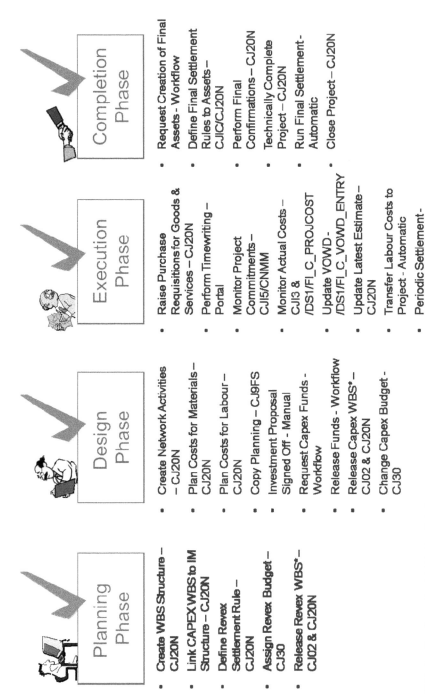

*Figure 1.10: Project process overview*

During the design phase, primarily planning activities take place, e.g. for labor and materials. During this phase, CAPEX funds for the execution phase are requested.

During the execution phase, purchase requisitions for goods & services are raised. Moreover, IAS 16 requires that time writing is performed. Time writing is executed using the CATS (Cross Application Time Sheet) application. This application is used to post the working hours directly against project codes. It enables the project manager and the project controller to track the project staff costs. Labor bookings are also an accounting requirement from the previously mentioned IAS 16, which demands a full cost approach including staff costs. Staff costs are always a topic in benchmarking large projects, but more importantly are a key topic in the investment proposal.

I will explain the CATS application in deeper detail in section 3.4 Execution Phase".

The focus for the completion and handover phase is on preparing to close out the project within SAP. Asset master data must be requested. The technical completion of the project must be prepared with an enormous data cleansing effort with regard to open commitments. After that, all WBS elements and all networks must be closed (status CLSD) in SAP.

At this point, we have an understanding of how SAP is set up for investment planning and controlling purposes. Moreover, I have provided the types of projects that can be set up in SAP-PS, the funding fundamentals, and most importantly the project process as the main guidance throughout the whole book.

In the next chapter, I will cover the roles and responsibilities of individuals working in projects, which is primarily important with regard to governance and compliance topics, as not every individual has the same role within the project especially in regards to responsibility for budgets.

# 2   Project Process Overview

In this chapter, I will explain the relevant roles and responsibilities and their set up in SAP. There are at least seven different roles available during the project process. I will list them first and then go through a detailed explanation.

## 2.1   Roles & Responsibilities

### Manage and Control IM Budget

The incumbent can update the IM budget for the relevant class of business and manage the funding. He/she is able to run Business Warehouse reports on the program level. However, the incumbent cannot release the budget from IM to the project system (SAP-PS). This role will be mapped to global CAPEX planners who will manage the IM budgets per class of business. This role should not be mapped to project managers. The incumbent is the owner of the IM structure per class of business.

### Plan and Rank Initiatives (budget holder)

A single Investment Management (IM) structure is created by Class of Business (global not country-specific). Each IM structure has a person assigned as agreed by the global CoB organization. The individual in this role receives an email request for the release of CAPEX to a project and will need to approve budget release via the SAP Portal. The approval done by the incumbent is the final release as all project / investment decision approvals should have happened prior to this stage outside of SAP. The funding process is completely carried out outside of SAP. The investment proposal, which briefly describes the scope of the project and also contains the economics, as well as possible alternatives, is a written document. This document is circulated within the authorized parties, which contains senior leaders only. Moreover this document contains a cash-flow forecast and brief visualization of the effects of the project on the profit and loss account and within the balance sheet. A capital project cannot incur actual expenditures or raise purchasing commitments unless budget has been allocated within the WBS structure.

## Report Programs

The incumbent primarily reviews budget or actual reports at high level project or program levels (across projects, not detailed level within single projects). Typically, a management accountant is in charge of management information reporting. The role has access to both SAP R/3 and BW reports with focus on analysis rather than project operational support. The incumbents could be from any of the following organizations e.g. business finance, management accountant, fixed asset accountant, etc. (but not project managers). This role could be mapped to senior project or program managers who require reporting across multiple projects for a class of business (e.g. in a region).

## Manage Project Reference Data

This role is mapped to global master record data focal points only (no local mapping). The incumbent maintains:

- ▶ WBS templates in SAP
- ▶ WBS spend types in SAP
- ▶ Global IM structures

The incumbent is the person responsible for the table, in line with the manual of authorities. The manual of authorities clarifies who has the authority to sign invoices and up to which amount. It is the basis for the enterprise on how segregation of duties is carried out within the organization.

The role reassigns level 1 WBS elements to different IM positions and is responsible for the processing of the IM first of the year tasks in SAP.

## Maintain Project Structures

This is a typical project administrator role to support the project manager and project financial management. For example, a business finance role for direct asset purchasing, asset retirement obligation (ARO) projects, cost recovery and statistical projects or process cost reporting. This could also be used for 3rd Party access. This role does not have as much authorization as the project manager. The incumbent cannot release funds to a project from IM and assign REVEX budget to a project. The role is allowed to raise purchase requisitions from the project and update the value of work done (VOWD) for the project.

## Manage and Control Projects

This is a primarily a project manager role for project management and execution. The individual cannot release CAPEX budget to the project from IM to PS. They are able to make purchase requisitions from the project and to manage purchasing commitments. In addition, this role can update project plan values and copy plans between projects. Moreover, the person responsible is able to release the project structure once funds have been allocated to it (CAPEX). It is also possible to allocate the REVEX budget to REVEX WBS elements and update the project structures, latest estimate figures, and settlement rules, etc. So typically this role is assigned to either project managers or project engineers, corporate functions (IT / HR / CP / HSSE, Finance), GAME Turnaround project managers, or engineers.

## Report Projects

This role has access to SAP R/3 and BW reports for plan / actual, budget, and commitment project reporting. Access to line item reporting for detailed analysis purposes is also included.

This role is assigned to all project managers and project administrators and may be required by project or program accountants.

## 2.2   Create master record data request

Figure 2.1 shows the process flow for the master data request. This process is mainly carried out in shared services because they are responsible for creating new record data. The red pillars are processed as workflows in an application called universal work list (UWL). Blue pillars represent manual process parts, and the orange pillar is carried out directly in SAP.

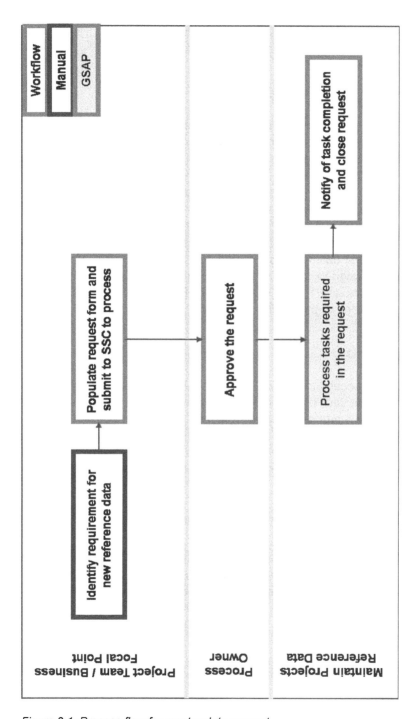

*Figure 2.1: Process flow for master data request*

# 3 Project Process

**The project process was illustrated in Figure 1.10. Now I will explain this process in more detail.**

## 3.1 Overview

First I would like to repeat the four standard phases characteristic for the project process. In chorological order:

- ▶ Planning phase
- ▶ Design phase
- ▶ Execution phase
- ▶ Completion phase

For each phase, we will discuss the activities and relevant SAP transactions along with their impact on controlling activities. Starting with a brief glance at the setup of the process and the roles and responsibilities as stated in Section 2.1 – here are some more assumptions. This setup has an important impact on project engineers responsible for the operational and system part of the projects. This requires proper technical skills in the business.

Furthermore the controlling piece on investment, which is a classical finance task, is increasingly being shifted towards the business side.

Currently project structure (WBS) is set up late in the process, i.e. once CAPEX approval is available.

### Create projects in SAP early

To avoid hiccups it is necessary to create projects in SAP in the very early stages to capture REVEX / CAPEX on the project level.

The Automatic Purchase Order process is triggered by SAP-PS: this means that no Contracting and Procurement-review of standard catalogue material takes place during the project execution. Therefore, high quality master data is required.

## 3.2  Planning Phase

Figure 3.1 illustrates the activities executed in SAP during the planning phase.

- **Create WBS Structure – CJ20N**
- **Link CAPEX WBS to IM Structure – CJ20N**
- **Define Revex Settlement Rule – CJ20N**
- **Assign Revex Budget – CJ30**
- **Release Revex WBS – CJ02 & CJ20N**

*Figure 3.1: Activities during the planning phase*

Activities during the planning phase are primarily executed in the Project Builder. In SAP this application can be called up using transaction code CJ20N. The WBS structure is setup and linked to the already existing IM structure. Settlement rules for the REVEX elements must be defined. These types of elements only settle expenses to the profit and loss account. If there are expenditures that result in a fixed asset, the expenditures, e.g. for pre-payments, have to be adjusted via manual journal entries later on.

After receiving the confirmed investment proposal the budget has to be allocated to the WBS elements. Last but not least, the newly created WBS's must be released via transaction CJ02.

Now I would like to elaborate further on the necessary activities within PS. Let's take a closer look at the Project Builder default settings. Figure 3.2 illustrates the entry screen for the Project Builder. The application opens in edit mode by default. So it can be useful to change it to open in display mode.

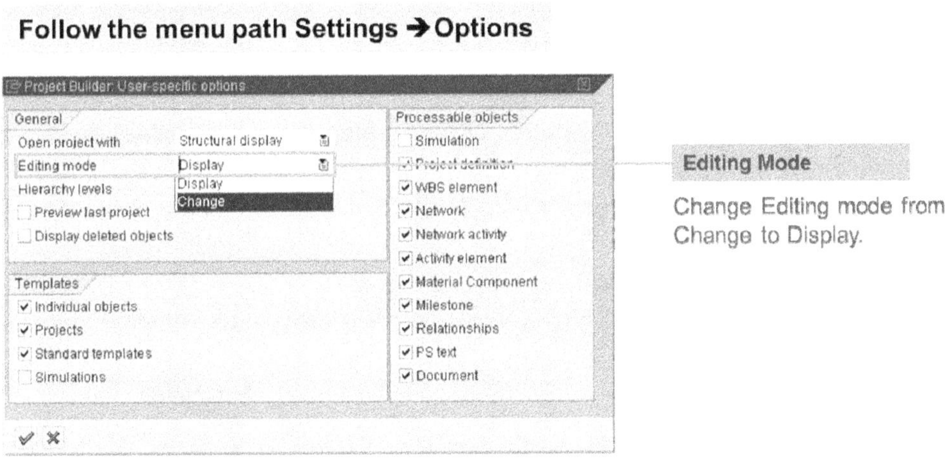

**Follow the menu path Settings → Options**

*Figure 3.2: Project Builder default settings*

The following Figure 3.3 demonstrates how to change the settings to open in display mode. Select transaction code CJ20N, and then select a Project Definition, a WBS element or a network activity number. Then, that select the display mode as shown in Figure 3.3.

## Follow the menu path Settings →Options

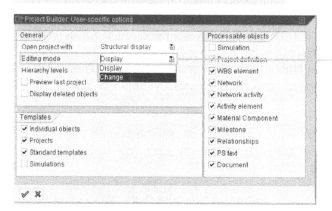

Projects will now open in display mode.
This allows you to select the WBS you wish to work on before selecting change mode. *☺*
By working in this manner you will not lock the whole of the project and so other users will be able to process other areas of the project at the same time.

*Figure 3.3: How to change to display mode*

Once the default is changed, projects will now open in display mode. This allows the user to select the WBS level to work on before changing the selected mode. By working in this manner the user will not lock the whole project, so that other users are able to process other areas of the project structure at the same time.

Figure 3.4 shows how to select the displayed hierarchy level of the project.

## Follow the menu path Settings →Options

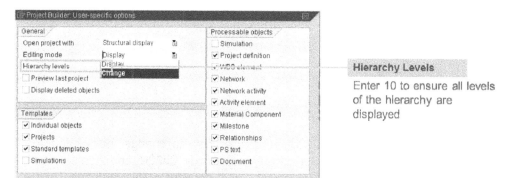

**Hierarchy Levels**

Enter 10 to ensure all levels of the hierarchy are displayed

*Figure 3.4: Changing the displayed hierarchy levels*

If the user prefers to have all levels displayed, they must enter ten digits. Then, all of the entered elements down to the network activities will be displayed. If this level of detail is unnecessary or seldom used, it can easily be changed.

The last detail that should be mentioned here is the preview option for the last edited project as illustrated in Figure 3.5.

## Follow the menu path Settings ➔ Options

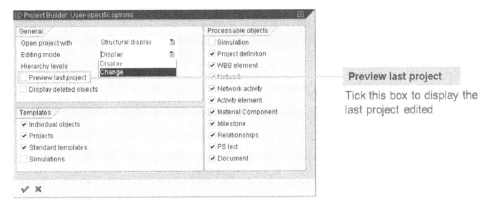

**Preview last project**

Tick this box to display the last project edited

*Figure 3.5: Last edited project preview.*

Now I would like to take a more detailed glance at the project structure. Figure 3.6 illustrates a typical project structure and I will explain some default settings that you should enter into the system.

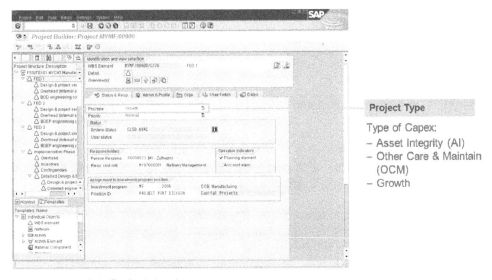

**Project Type**

Type of Capex:
- Asset Integrity (AI)
- Other Care & Maintain (OCM)
- Growth

*Figure 3.6: Project structure*

35

There are three types of projects:

- ▶ Asset integrity projects
- ▶ Other care and maintain
- ▶ Growth

Asset integrity projects are also called revamps or life time extension projects. Usually they are directly linked to the license to operate, which means that these projects are primarily executed due to new legislative issues; e.g. the German Bundesimmisionsschutzgesetz (BimSchG), or the protection of water and land. Not executing these projects can either result in fines or even closing the business. Due to IFRS guidelines, these projects are usually investment projects.

**Asset integrity projects**

Asset integrity projects are typically directly linked to a license to operate. Improperly executing the project can result in fines or business closure.

Other care and maintain projects is a category used for maintenance projects. As this book is focused on investments, I mention maintenance projects for informational purposes only.

The last category primarily covers investment projects because growth projects mostly deal with building completely new assets. These types of projects indicate a substantial increase on profit and operations, with a direct effect as well on B/S and P/L.

Figure 3.7 illustrates the link between the project and the funds in IM. The purpose of this link is to make the funds available and to enable project monitoring project on the IM level as well. Another entry is used to link the project location to an identification number in the IM module.

Probably the most important entry is the investment profile. The investment profile determines the type of asset under construction number that will be automatically created when the CAPEX WBS containing an account assignment is released. The investment profile is a default from the chosen WBS template. REVEX investment profiles must be left blank

**unless** a low value asset is going to be created that will need to be capitalized for local statutory purposes. In this case, the investment profile Z00600 – GSAP; PP&E Group Only, must be chosen. The entry for the investment profile is illustrated in Figure 3.8.

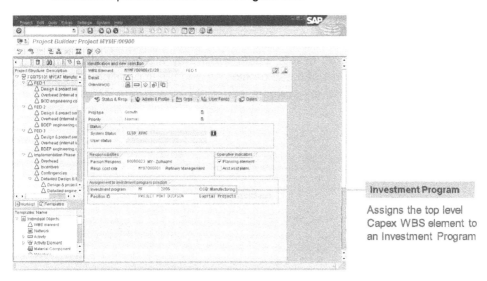

**Investment Program**

Assigns the top level Capex WBS element to an Investment Program

*Figure 3.7: Project structure linked to IM on the top level*

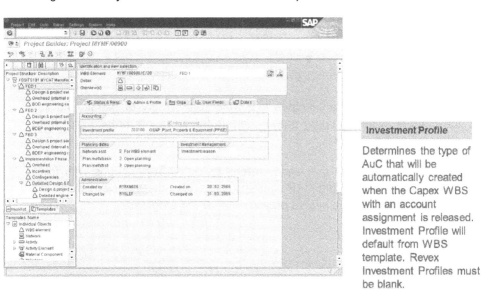

**Investment Profile**

Determines the type of AuC that will be automatically created when the Capex WBS with an account assignment is released. Investment Profile will default from WBS template. Revex Investment Profiles must be blank.

*Figure 3.8: Investment profiles entry*

For accounting purposes, SAP has to provide several types of investment profiles. Some accounting principles, like low value assets in Germany, are often unknown internationally. Low value assets are small
assets with a value lower than 410- Euros. Figure 3.9 illustrates the
available investment profiles. Investment profiles should only to be used
for CAPEX WBS elements. Low value assets require a REVEX WBS
element and an investment profile. In German statutory accounting these
items are represented as assets, under IFRS they are costs within the
P/L-account. The majority of these profiles are the result of differences in
German and international tax systems, especially for software issues.

Z00100 - GSAP; Plant, Property and Equipment (PP&E)

Z00200 - GSAP; Software Internally Developed

Z00300 - GSAP; Software Acquired thr. Business Combination

Z00400 - GSAP; Software Acquired / Purchased Others

Z00500 - GSAP; Turnaround

Z00600 - GSAP; PP&E Group Only

Z00700 - GSAP: PP&E Tax only

Z00800 – Direct Capital Purchase (statistical)

*Figure 3.9: Investment profiles overview*

There are two important entries left, which are worthy of mentioning in
the context of the planning phase. One is the legacy reference and the
other is the spend type.

Figure 3.10 illustrates the legacy reference entry. This topic is very important when the current SAP system (also called the legacy system) is
updated, but already contains projects that are in progress.

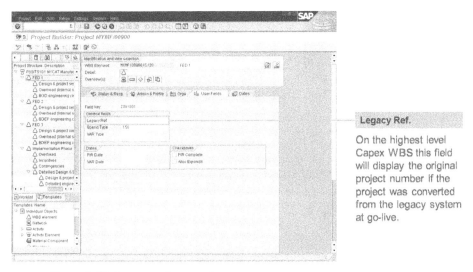

*Figure 3.10: Legacy reference 1*

Figure 3.11 illustrates the spend type entry. This entry provides a high level of project spend categorization and is used for project reporting purposes. The available selections will depend on the project profit center and is mandatory for level 1 CAPEX WBS only. Moreover, the spend type depends on the project types as mentioned previously. For example, the spend type for a growth project would differ from the spend type of an asset integrity project.

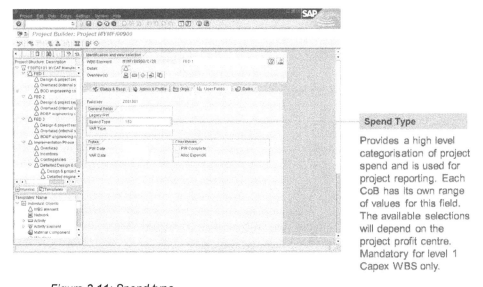

*Figure 3.11: Spend type*

## 3.3 Design Phase

Figure 3.12 contains a short recap of the activities executed during the design phase. Design is another term for changing the outer appearance of the assets as build during the projects, e.g. the routing of pipelines or the size of the new stack.

- **Create Network Activities – CJ20N**
- **Plan Costs for Materials – CJ20N**
- **Plan Costs for Labour – CJ20N**
- **Copy Planning – CJ9FS**
- **Investment Proposal Signed Off - Manual**
- **Request Capex Funds - Workflow**
- **Release Funds - Workflow**
- **Release Capex WBS – CJ02 & CJ20N**
- **Change Capex Budget - CJ30**

*Figure 3.12: Design phase*

The network activities are created in the design phase. This is the first step towards the procurement process because the network activities are used to create purchase requisitions, which will later on be transferred into a purchase order.

40

Figure 3.13 illustrates the four types of network activities available in the Project Builder work list.

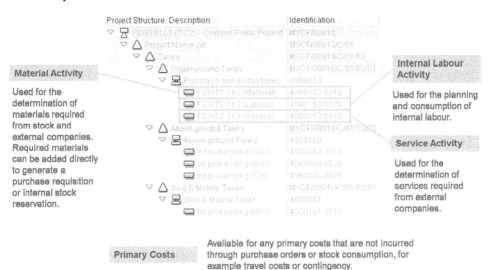

**Material Activity**

Used for the determination of materials required from stock and external companies. Required materials can be added directly to generate a purchase requisition or internal stock reservation.

**Internal Labour Activity**

Used for the planning and consumption of internal labour.

**Service Activity**

Used for the determination of services required from external companies.

**Primary Costs**

Available for any primary costs that are not incurred through purchase orders or stock consumption, for example travel costs or contingency.

*Figure 3.13 Types of network activities*

As mentioned before there are four types of network activities:

► Material activities

► Service activities

► Internal labor activities

► Primary cost activities

Material activities are used for the determination of materials required either from stock or from external vendors. Required materials can be added directly to generate a purchase requisition or an internal stock reservation.

Service activities are used for the determination of services required from external vendors.

Internal labor activities are used for the planning and consumption of internal resources. Moreover IAS 16 requires a full cost approach. So the internal labor costs are part of the capitalized assets resulting from investment projects.

41

Primary costs activities are available for any primary costs that are not incurred through purchase orders or stock consumption, for example travel costs or contingency.

There are some defaults that have to be taken into account when purchasing materials and services. Materials and services should not be requested together in the same activity. The requisition approver has to be in line with the amount noted in the current manual of authorities. Additional text should be added for generic materials and services, in order to specify what kind of service or equipment should be ordered. The purchasing group is entered at the line item level when the request needs to go to another buyer other than your default. The purchasing group can either be a regional clustering, or include staff from the purchasing department, which is clustered in groups for certain technical disciplines, e.g. piping or scaffolding. Unloading point is a required field and initializes the warehouse shuttle service to the construction site.

Figure 3.14 illustrates the process flow for necessary activities, how to create either a service or a material activity. I like to compare it to an online shopping process.

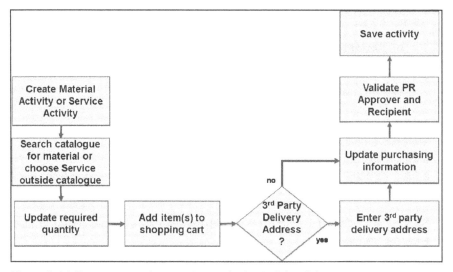

*Figure 3.14: Process overview create service/material activity*

The next topic I would like to introduce is procuring limit services. Again there are some requirements for this process, which I provide in the following part of this chapter.

Limited services cannot be selected from the equipment catalogue as offered in SAP, free text and the reference to a frame contract is mandatory. The contract number is entered into the service activity screen. After that, the expected value and value limit are both entered. The expected value and the committed value of the purchase order are a little bit different. The expected value is a planning figure for internal purposes, whereas the committed value is represented to the vendor. The value limit or overall limit is the maximum value that can be entered at service receipt and basis for requisition approval. The purchasing group defaults from the contract.

This can differ either from site to site or within the different business clusters. In the case of procuring materials, the default material group (procuring goods and services coding) is mandatory. The long text in the requisition must include a detailed description of the service. You or the vendor will select the detail of the services performed after the work is completed on the service entry sheet.

Figure 3.15 illustrates the process flow for procuring limit services at one glance.

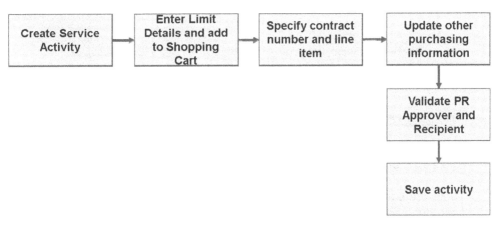

*Figure 3.15: Create limit service request*

There is some additional purchasing information required, which differs according to whether you are ordering generic or catalogued material. This information tackles the three topics price, long text and vendor. Figure 3.16 illustrates the aforementioned topics and the two different purchasing processes.

| | *Generic Material* | *Catalogued Material* | |
|---|---|---|---|
| Price | Enter estimated price | Cannot be changed - firm price | |
| Long Text | Enter exact description | Not required | |
| Vendor | Optional | Cannot be changed - firm source | |

*Figure 3.16: Additional purchasing information*

If you have any changes or variations in your project, it may be unavoidable to change or even delete activities. Ideally the purchase requisition has not been changed into a purchase order. Figure 3.17 illustrates the activities necessary to change or cancel an activity.

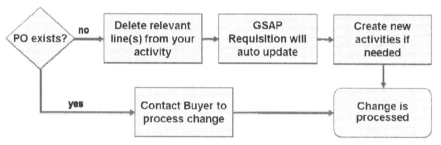

*Figure 3.17: Change or cancel activities*

There are some additional default settings with regard to the purchasing user, but I would like to emphasize just two of them that are important to understand when we are talking about external procurement. First, the entry of the purchase requisition approver should be directly linked to the manual of authorities, which is mandatory for the business in which the project is executed. Second, I would like to stress the correct entry of the unloading point. It might be possible, for example, for a project executed in a chemical plant for there to be more than one warehouse that could receive the material ordered. For this reason, it is essential that an easy logistical connection to the project area is available. All necessary entries are demonstrated in the following Figure 3.18 and Figure 3.19.

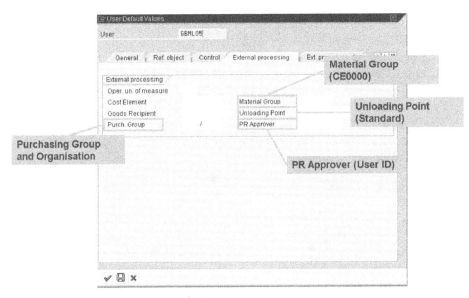

*Figure 3.18: Purchasing user defaults*

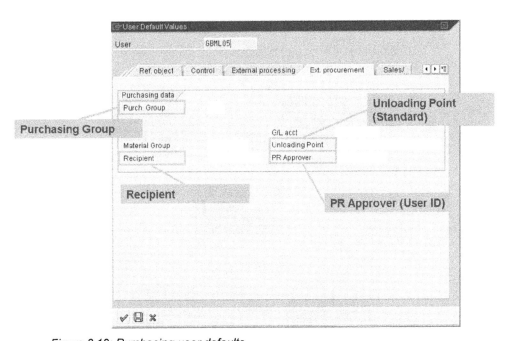

*Figure 3.19: Purchasing user defaults*

One interesting point I would like to mention is the fact that there is the possibility of copying already existing activities and using them with minor changes, e.g. another vendor. The only way to save versions is with planned detailed requisitions. This may prove to be too detailed at early stages of development to save as versions. Early planning will be completed outside of SAP and can be saved as versions when the actual requirements are better known. This functionality provides the ability to report on previous plan versions that contain information for different project phases.

Common Plan Versions:

▶ **FID:** Final Investment Decision (approx. +/- 10% cost estimating accuracy)

▶ **P20:** Second Cut Design (approx. +/- 20% cost estimating accuracy)

▶ **P30:** Initial Front-end Design (approx. +/- 30% cost estimating accuracy

A good rule of thumb is that the accuracy improves with each plan version and is nearly +/- 0% when the final funds are requested.

Figure 3.20 illustrates the approval process for capitalized expenditures, which as mentioned before takes place outside SAP.

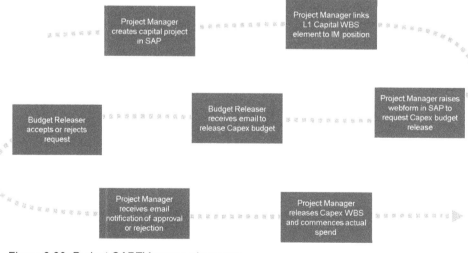

*Figure 3.20: Project CAPEX approval process*

As I have already mentioned, Figure 3.20 demonstrates that some typical finance activities are shifted to more technically oriented staff, e.g. the project manager who is able to create the project setup in SAP.

It is the project manager's responsibility to link level 1 WBS elements to the relevant IM position in order to make the project funds available. The PM also submits a request via web form in SAP to request the CAPEX budget release. This topic will be elaborated on in subsequent sections. After the funds are successfully released, the PM is informed via email. Then they can release the CAPEX WBS's and start to request and order services and materials for the project.

Figure 3.21 illustrates the aforementioned web request form, which is a mandatory step towards final funding.

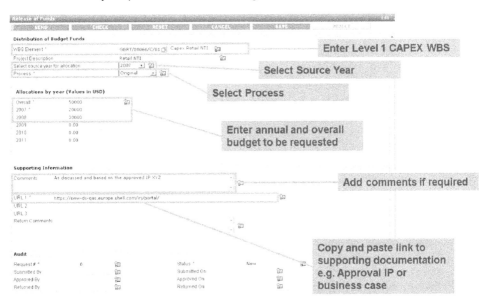

*Figure 3.21: CAPEX budget request via web form in SAP*

I would like to highlight two interesting points in regards to Figure 3.21.

The web form offers the opportunity to enter both the annual and the overall requested budgets. You can also embed a link with supporting documentation, e.g. the approved IP or the underlying business case. This might be relevant to create a proper audit trail, especially if regular job rotation is part of "your" business model. To avoid information from getting lost, it is key to have a proper and up to date documentation. This is an important topic, especially when it comes to onboarding new staff.

47

## 3.4 Execution Phase

After the design is finished and all relevant technical drawings (as build documentation) are available, all contract negotiations are closed out and the staffing is complete. Thereafter follows the execution phase, which means realization of the project in the field. Figure 3.22 shows the relevant SAP activities.

Execution
Phase

* **Raise Purchase
  Requisitions for Goods &
  Services – CJ20N**
* **Perform Timewriting –
  Portal**
* **Monitor Project
  Commitments –
  CJI5/CNMM**
* **Monitor Actual Costs –
  CJI3 &
  /DS1/FI_C_PROJCOST**
* **Update VOWD -
  /DS1/FI_C_VOWD_ENTRY**
* **Update Latest Estimate –
  CJ20N**
* **Transfer Labour Costs to
  Project - Automatic**
* **Periodic Settlement -
  Automatic**

*Figure 3.22: SAP activities in the execution phase*

Let's take a closer look at activities in the execution phase.

At this point, the necessary funding for the project is done and services and materials can be requested via SAP. Another very important task during this phase is the time writing for the project team members. This is carried out in an application directly linked to SAP, which is called CATS. CATS is an abbreviation for Cross Application Time Sheet.

Direct time writing is only carried out for full time staff. This is an IAS 16 requirement, which demands a full cost approach. This also includes the costs for full time staff working on investment projects. I will give a more detailed explanation of CATS in the course of this chapter.

Regular controlling tasks during execution are the monitoring of outstanding commitments and actual costs, as well as the monthly updating of the value of work done (VOWD) and the latest estimate (LE), which is part of the business plan.

Last but not least, two automatic queries are carried out monthly at a minimum. These are the transferring of labor costs posted via CATS, and the periodic settlement (transaction code CJ 88) of the project actuals costs from the project module (SAP-PS) to the finance module (SAP-FI).

After this brief introduction, I will elaborate further on each of the topics mentioned above.

I will start with how to create a purchase requisition. Figure 3.23 illustrates this process and illustrates the mandatory information needed for the contracting and procurement departments.

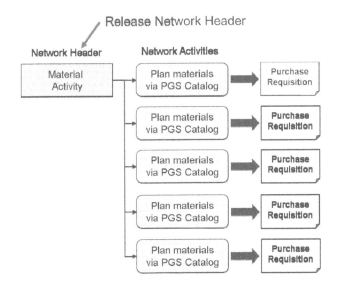

*Figure 3.23: The process of creating a purchase requisition*

The process demonstrated in Figure 3.23 indicates that purchase orders (PO) are automatically delivered, the approved requisition for specified catalogue material will automatically generate and process PO: no contracting and procurement review takes place for standard material.

What about the risk of assigning the incorrect requisition (e.g. materials instead of services) to WBS? It is technically possible that that the material master will be linked to a service activity and the other way around (by mistake). In the event that you are purchasing equipment via a service activity, you will lose track because there is only one goods received posting. But usually you have certain steps, including pre-fabrication of large equipment or partial delivery. For example, you order ten pumps, but get them delivered in five steps, two at a time. The delivery date in SAP will be the latest possible date, in the worst case scenario the work will not be able to be done because of the late delivery of materials.

The next topic I would like to cover is time writing. Cross Application Time Sheet (CATS) are used for time capture. This procedure is mandatory for internal staff working on CAPEX projects. Exception time (e.g. leave) will continue to be entered by full time staff. The entry will be made via SAP. It is important to mention that no approval is required for time booked to projects – project managers are responsible for reviewing reports and making adjustments as necessary. The internal charge out rate used will be by job group and calculated locally. The internal charge out rate is an average of all available job groups and the related salary and wages. It is comparable to an hourly rate charged for contracted staff.

Time can be written to various accounting elements including:

► Cost Centers
► Networks
► Cost Centers and Statistical WBS Elements simultaneously

Figure 3.24 illustrates two mandatory entries: the activity for the accounting assignment and the sending cost center, which represents the department/ discipline where the staff is based. The cost center is a default regarding salary and wages, which is taken from the Human Resources (HR) record.

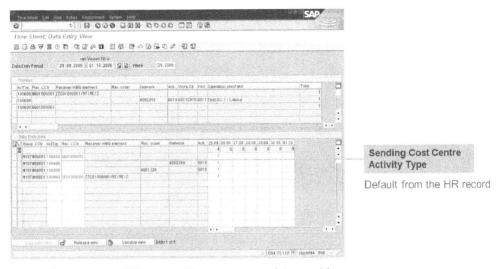

*Figure 3.24: CATS time writing screen mandatory entries*

Figure 3.25 shows the receiving cost center. This cost center is either the unit or venue where the project is carried out, or a cost center especially set up for the project. This is shown in Figure 3.25. Moreover there can be other receiving objects, like work orders or WBS elements.

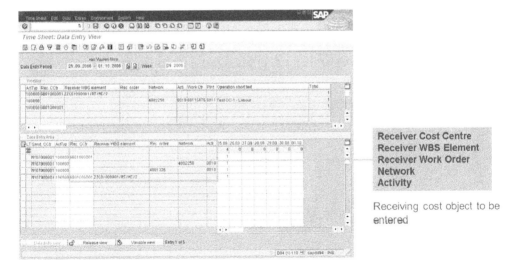

*Figure 3.25: CATS time writing receiving cost objects*

Figure 3.26 illustrates the dates that need to be entered into CATS. A calendar window pops up and allows you to enter the hours worked on the project on a daily basis. The dates must be updated at least on a monthly basis for month-end closing purposes. Time writing is an important component within the VOWD, which includes actual costs and accruals for services and materials received, but not yet invoiced.

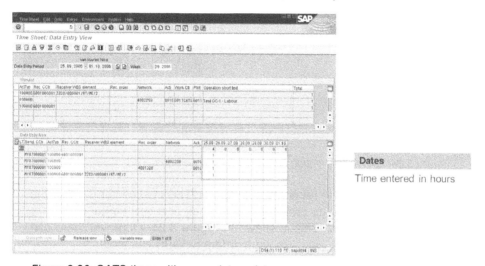

*Figure 3.26: CATS time writing mandatory dates*

To simplify the monthly inputs SAP-CATS offers the opportunity to copy previous entries. These previous entries are stored in the work list demonstrated in Figure 3.27.

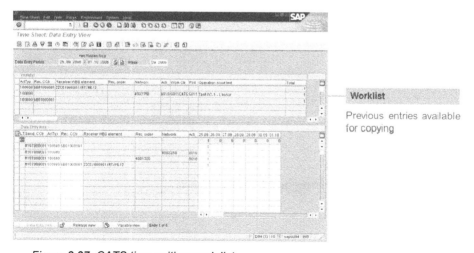

*Figure 3.27: CATS time writing work list*

52

The next point I want to highlight is the management and monitoring of commitments during the execution phase. Once a purchase requisition is entered in SAP, the assigned budget is blocked and no longer available for the project. The same is true for a purchase order. Therefore, it is essential to monitor commitments on a regular basis, at the very least monthly. If a PO is redundant, immediate action from the project controller is required. The PM/Project Controller needs to inform the contracting and procurement department in order to close the PO and even more importantly, reduce the PO amount to zero. After that the money is again available for the project. Figure 3.28 states the process flow and the related actions concerning the monitoring of commitments.

Is the outstanding commitment still valid?

Have the goods/services been received?

Are additional Materials/services required?

Are line items coded incorrectly?

Should any commitments be carried forward?

*Figure 3.28: Process flow manage commitments*

I previously mentioned the importance of particular actions to ensure the accuracy of the month end close. One of the most important concepts in monthly closing activities is the VOWD accrual. First, I would like to explain the necessity of this concept. During the course of a project there might well be services and materials received, but not invoiced before month end. The relevant amount is a known entity because it is directly linked to purchase orders and frame contracts. So for closing purposes an accrual has to be posted.

Secondly, I would like to explain the mathematics behind this accrual. The formula for the VOWD accrual is as follows:

VOWD accrual = (PO order value/100 * VOWD percentage)
– actual costs

A simple example is illustrated in Figure 3.29 using the following information:

- ▶ PO order value: 100 k€
- ▶ Actual cost: 50 k€
- ▶ VOWD percentage: 80%

**(PO Order Value / 100 * VOWD percentage) – Actual cost**

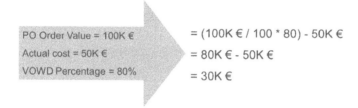

PO Order Value = 100K €
Actual cost = 50K €
VOWD Percentage = 80%

= (100K € / 100 * 80) - 50K €
= 80K € - 50K €
= 30K €

*Figure 3.29: Value of work done accrual*

In the example, the relevant accrual has to be posted for 30 k€. If the expected actuals are invoiced within the following period the accrual will be reversed automatically from SAP and replaced by actual costs. To ensure the accuracy of this accrual, the posting has to be done on the basis of every single purchase order relating to the project.

Figure 3.30 illustrates the entry screen for this accrual.

There are some additional facts to take into consideration. The underlying accounting process for accruals like VOWD needs to be aligned with internal controls. It is required to provide back up to accruals for auditors, especially at quarter end and year end, e.g. print and sign with date by project manager. Thus a proper audit trail will be set up.

Accounting is not the only piece that will be updated during month end close, it is also mandatory to update the latest estimate reporting with essential data in order to update the phasing of costs with regard to delays or in case of undecided claims. Figure 3.31 illustrates the LE updating process as an iceberg model, which assumes that most of the recognition might not be viable at first glance.

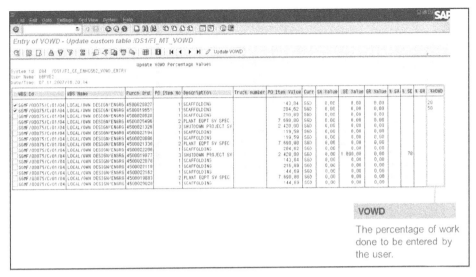

*Figure 3.30: VOWD entry screen*

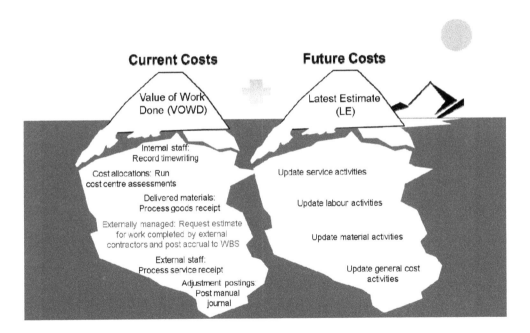

*Figure 3.31: Updating of project costs iceberg model*

To show how all of the aforementioned activities fit together, I have in-cluded Figure 3.32 to show the month end process as a whole.

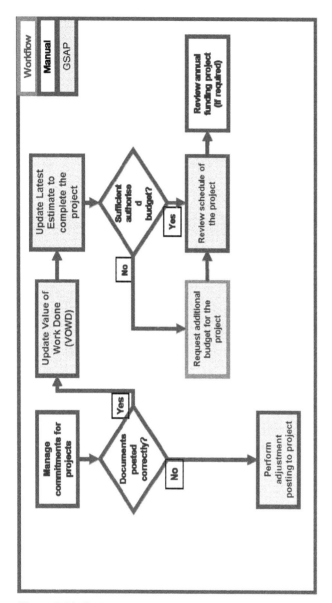

*Figure 3.32: Project controls at month end*

## 3.5   Completion Phase

Let's now look at activities executed during the completion phase of an investment project.

- Request Creation of Final Assets - Workflow
- Define Final Settlement Rules to Assets – CJIC/CJ20N
- Perform Final Confirmations – CJ20N
- Technically Complete Project – CJ20N
- Run Final Settlement - Automatic
- Close Project – CJ20N

*Figure 3.33: Completion phase activities*

The assets built during the course of the project are nearly finished so a request needs to be issued to create the final asset within the SAP asset accounting module (FI-AA). This can be done via workflow.

Prior to this request, the final settlement rules for the asset need to be defined. This is a mandatory requirement and requires special attention, especially since the component approach from IAS 16 is mandatory for proper asset accounting. This means that every single asset has to be split up in its significant components, for example a chemical plant might comprise of foundations, vessels, valves, heat exchangers, and pipe-lines, etc. All of this equipment might have different economic lifetimes and moreover, different depreciation rules. Additionally there might be differences in statutory accounting in large enterprises, group accounting treatments, etc.

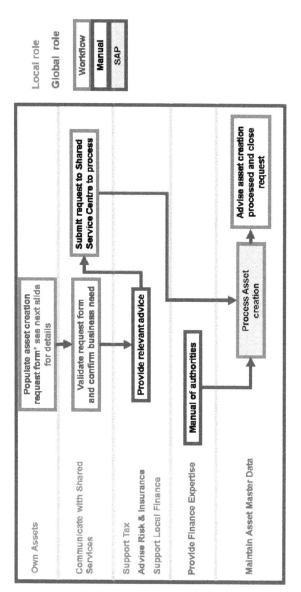

*Figure 3.34: Create asset master data*

All these aforementioned requests need separate confirmations, due to segregation of duties. All of these activities are carried out in the Project Builder application with activity code CJ20N. Figure 3.35 illustrates the process flow regarding the asset creation. In order to process this request properly it is essential for the project to have a complete list containing all final componentized assets at hand. This list should be in line with the scope as of the IP. The request for the asset creation requires the approval of the asset owner. This role is usually assigned to the production unit manager (relevant for a Brownfield project) or the leader of the entity (in case of a Greenfield project).

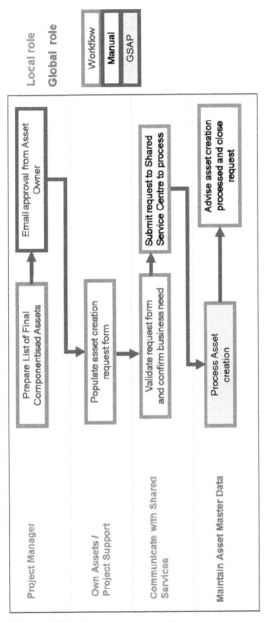

*Figure 3.35: Trigger asset creation*

Figure 3.36 illustrates the finance data request, which includes the specific entry data in order to maintain asset master data appropriately.

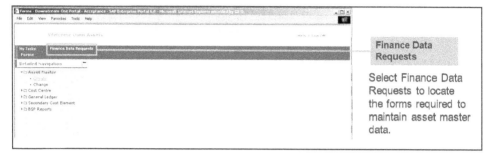

*Figure 3.36: Finance data requests*

Figure 3.37 illustrates the entry screen for the asset master requests containing the applicable options. This is a workflow transaction carried out in a web form which has an interface to SAP.

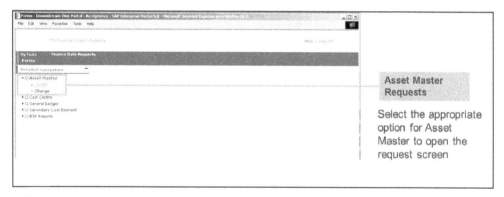

*Figure 3.37: Asset master requests*

In the following figures, I would like to show the header data required in the asset master data process to ensure proper accounting treatment.

First of all, the asset needs a correct allocation to an asset class as shown below in Figure 3.38. The asset class determines several mandatory input data, like the G/L account, depreciation terms (to steer the useful economic life), and the definition of the asset master records.

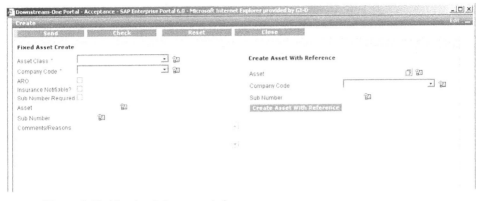

*Figure 3.38: Header data – asset class*

Figure 3.39 shows the input screen for the ARO (Asset retirement obligation), which can be a legal requirement for the entity in order to leave the
property as it was before starting operations, e.g. to remove a drilling
platform in the north sea or to repopulate a forest after finishing the mining operations. If the need to post an ARO crops up, it has to be part of
the investment proposal in order to meet legal prerequisites.

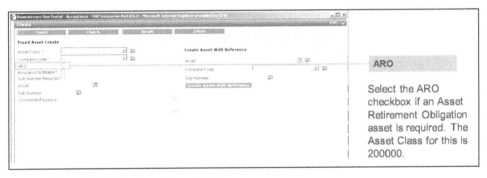

*Figure 3.39:  Header data – ARO*

Assets in chemical plants are often huge and complex. They are comprised of a collection of components including pumps, concrete, vessels,
heat exchangers, etc. These components are/might be parts of a complex machine like an ethylene plant. So these parts have to be registered
separately with regard to asset accounting, but also in light of carrying an
accurate stocktaking into exercise. Thus SAP must be up to date and
configured to provide lists that can be used during the stocktaking exercise.

Therefore asset sub-numbers are a crucial part of asset accounting and asset master data as well. The entry screen for this selection is shown in Figure 3.40 below.

*Figure 3.40:  Header data – asset & sub no.*

Last but not least there should be a meaningful description of the under-lying asset entered into the system, see Figure 3.41. After that all rele-vant information regarding asset master data is available.

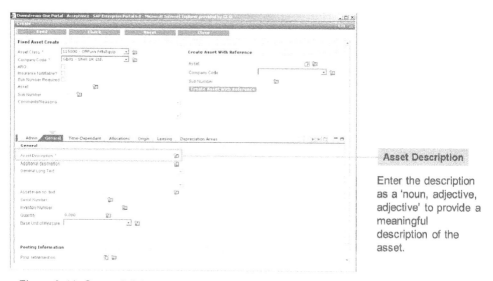

*Figure 3.41: General data*

The next topic I would like to look at is a sub-section of asset master data: time dependent data.

One important example regarding time dependent data is the right cost center, so that costs are charged to the production unit where the project is carried out. This fits also into the context of stocktaking, as every asset can also only be related to one cost center as illustrated in Figure 3.42. The relation to one cost center only ensures the right charging of later costs, e.g. from the depreciation.

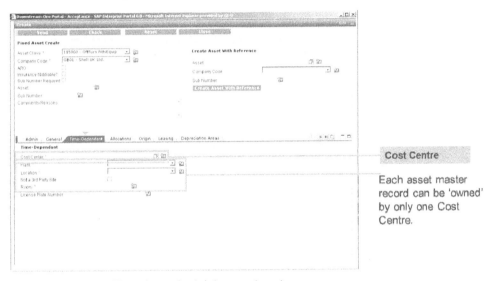

*Figure 3.42: Time dependent data – cost center*

Also important in light of stocktaking is data like plant, location and room. This data is indispensable for tangible assets, like printers or office equipment because there are usually a lot of them. If you want to find it back from report out of SAP you have to specify the location, e.g. where the printer physically is or to which production unit the equipment belongs.

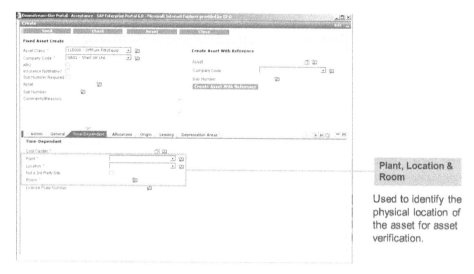

*Figure 3.43: Time dependent data – Plant, room*

In the next section, I will cover cost allocation. As I mentioned earlier, it is very important to link the asset to the correct asset class. Moreover, there might be differences between statutory accounting like German GAAP and international accounting like IFRS and tax requirements. Therefore, it is key to enter the data in the correct evaluation group. This is highlighted in Figure 3.44 below.

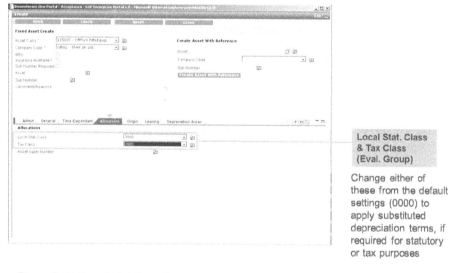

*Figure 3.44: Local statutory class*

If there is the need for an ARO posting, it is also possible to enter an asset super number. This enables you to break down a large plant into its components, as well as summarize the components back to the large plant (see Figure 3.45.)

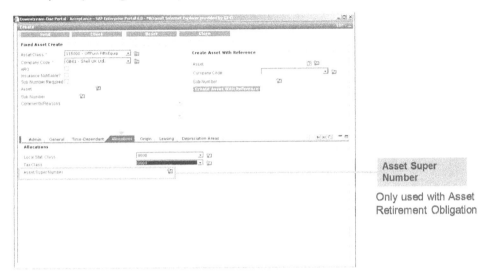

*Figure 3.45: Asset super number*

Besides the asset class, it is crucial to enter the right depreciation area (Local GAAP, IFRS, taxes, etc.), the depreciation key (method, e.g. straight-line) and the useful life of the asset. These data input varieties are shown below in Figure 3.46, Figure 3.47, and Figure 3.48.

From my experience as a project finance manager, it is key to resolve outstanding commitments, especially during the completion phase. First, the project controller has to identify the outstanding commitments and run a SAP-PS report using the transaction code CJI5. The discipline engineers then need to deal with the fact that either the goods and services were received, or not. If the ordered goods and services are already received, a receipt for goods/services has to be processed if required.

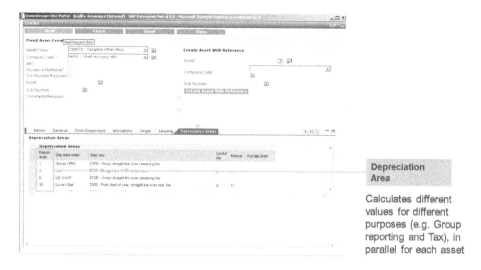

Figure 3.46: Depreciation areas

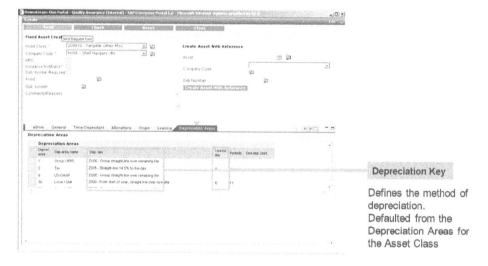

Figure 3.47: Depreciation keys

If the relevant goods and services have not been received during the completion phase it is key to elaborate if the commitments remain valid. If yes, the discipline lead has to follow up with the relevant purchaser. If not, the commitment has to be removed from the system. This can be done either in reducing the existing order, or in cancelling it completely.

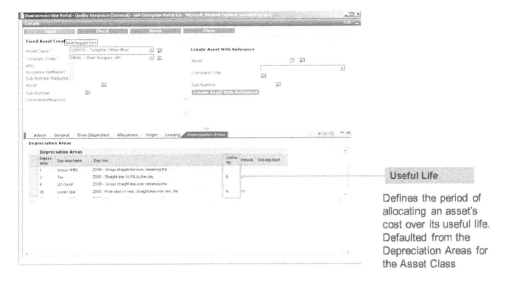

Useful Life

Defines the period of allocating an asset's cost over its useful life. Defaulted from the Depreciation Areas for the Asset Class

*Figure 3.48: Useful life*

Figure 3.49 illustrates the aforementioned actions as a possible process flow.

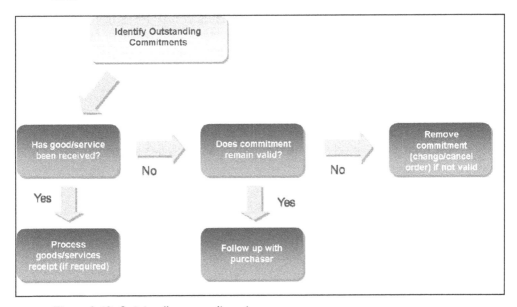

*Figure 3.49: Outstanding commitments*

67

The project has to be flagged as "technically complete" or in more technical terms the status TECO has to be set via the Project Builder (CJ20N).

I would like to explain the TECO status a bit more. When the project is flagged as TECO, new commitments cannot be created. Moreover, costs can only be posted for already outstanding commitments. Last but not least, this specific status has to be set for the cost elements to receive the costs during the settlement of costs during the periodic settlement run. If this activity fails the balance sheet presents a false statement with regard to fixed assets in the position property, plant, and equipment (PPE).

Additionally, there is another SAP-PS status. This is the status CLOSED (CLSD). The status is used as an internal indicator, if the project I still active or finished. Once the project has been flagged as CLOSED, it is no longer possible for the project to receive postings. All necessary activities to capitalize and close the project are shown in Figure 3.50.

**SAP PS CLOSED status**

The CLOSED (CLSD) status in SAP PS is used as an internal indicator, if the project I still active or finished. Once the project has been flagged as CLOSED, it is no longer possible for the project to receive postings.

Given the extensive amount of information covered in this chapter, let's review what we covered and the most important activities in each phase

## Planning Phase:

The WBS-structure is set up within SAP-PS. Moreover, the highest possible level of the project; the project definition in SAP-PS is linked with the related number in SAP-IM in order to make the budget available for the project.

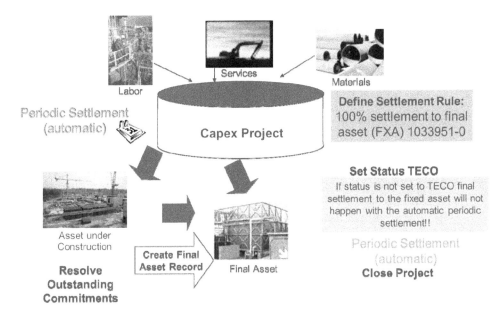

*Figure 3.50: Capitalize and close project*

## Design Phase:

In the design phase the next level below the WBS elements is set up. This level contains the network activities. These activities are used to create purchase requisitions, which are converted into purchase orders after the person responsible has confirmed that the purchase requisition is correct in SAP. These network activities are also used for planning topics covering labor and materials. The investment proposal (IP) is circulated through the organization in order to get the money/budget approved. After the IP is signed off and the money is available in SAP the budget is going to be allocated to the necessary level within the WBS-structure.

## Execution Phase:

The purchase orders are sent to the vendors in order to receive either services or materials as required to carry out the project scope. VOWD accruals must be posted with regard to the accounting requirements, as well as time writing has be done by staff working full time for the project.

The reporting of the latest estimate and the updating of the latest estimate are mandatory requirements also. Last but not least, regular settlement runs are carried out to charge the actual costs to the project WBS's.

## Completion Phase:

The assets masters must be created in SAP-AA to settle the costs from the project system to the accounting system. Settlement rules must be defined for each single asset as there can be differences in group accounting and statutory accounting. The status TECO (technically complete) has to be set, and a final settlement run must be provided. When the project has received the final costs the status has to be changed into CLSD (closed), so no one is able to generate additional costs for the project.

# 4 Project Scenarios

In this chapter, I would like to emphasize that there are many project scenarios for using SAP-PS beyond investment projects, although this should be the main purpose for project setup in SAP-PS.

## 4.1 Use of projects

The primary project profile is used to create development projects, which comprise of CAPEX and REVEX elements. Nevertheless, there are integrated scenarios possible where other process areas can be included. I want to highlight three of them:

Turnaround projects (Global Asset Manufacturing Excellence (GAME) process): As I mentioned in section 1.5 Types of Projects  turnarounds are large overhauls that need to be capitalized due to the accounting change in IAS 16. The related asset has a life time of five years (the typical TA cycle) and has to be settled via the straight-line method.

The next type of scenario is the statistical project for GAME, which is primarily used for internal maintenance works.

The third scenario is a direct asset purchase, or an intangible investment, for example if a car for the fire department is directly purchased.

With regard to complexity, the last type of scenario mentioned here are detailed project scenarios. I will introduce the four most common project scenarios used for these topics:

- ▶ Joint Venture (either entity managed or third party managed)
- ▶ ARO projects, i.e. mainly used for large decommissioning projects
- ▶ Cost recovery projects, i.e. cost allocation for intra group, third party, or associated entities
- ▶ Process cost reporting, i.e. mainly statistical project setup to make internal process costs viable.

## 4.2  Maintenance work order types

In Figure 3.4 I mentioned the types of cost elements that can be used within an investment project. Finally, I would like to look at maintenance work order types. As the name indicates, work orders should not be used within investment projects except to settle costs to WBS elements. Otherwise, these costs are not viable in the most common report used in projects, the OC1-sheet. Below I have listed a catalogue containing the different work order types. Only the MX06 is able to settle costs to a WBS element. So this is the only acceptable work order type within investment projects.

- ▶ MX01 = Mandated Preventive Maintenance Order without Notification
- ▶ MX02 = Mandated Preventive Maintenance Order with Notification
- ▶ MX03 = Conditioned Based and Non-Mandated PM Order
- ▶ MX04 = Reactive Maintenance Order
- ▶ MX05 = Administrative Maintenance Order
- ▶ MX06 = Project Work Order
- ▶ MX07 = Non-Routine Maintenance Order
- ▶ MX08 = Turnaround Maintenance Order
- ▶ MX09 = Maintenance Support to Operations Order
- ▶ MX10 = Proratables Order

Proratables is a technical term for the allocation of general costs, e.g. a scaffold is used by operations and a project at the same time. There has to be an allocation method to split the costs. So this type of order contains an allocation key to split the costs between operations and the project.

The other type of work order that can be used in investment projects is MX08 for Turnaround projects, which have to be capitalized under PPE as well as development projects.

## 4.3 GAME – TA (MX08) and project process (MX06)

In this section, I will cover the turnaround process and the deviations with regard to the project process. One of the most striking deviations between a turnaround event and a project is due to the fact that a turnaround event includes lots of bulk maintenance work. For this reason, it is key to use work orders which include all of the relevant planning data. The advantage of using work orders is that it is much easier to shift data and planning costs instead of using WBS elements and network activities. The process flow as integrated part of the GAME process is shown in Figure 4.1. In parallel to assigning work orders to relevant WBS elements, the request for asset master data creation is processed. This is a mandatory requirement because turnaround events usually take place within three or four weeks.

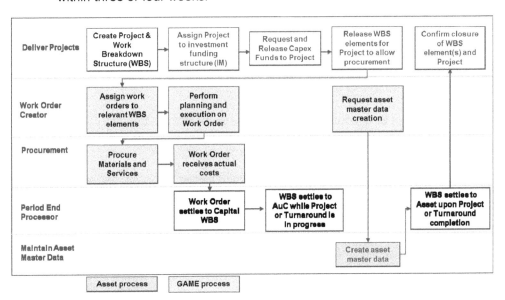

Figure 4.1: GAME – TA and project process

## 4.4 TA work order – assignment to WBS

Figure 4.2 shows how to assign a work order to a WBS element in the Project Builder application (transaction code CJ20N).

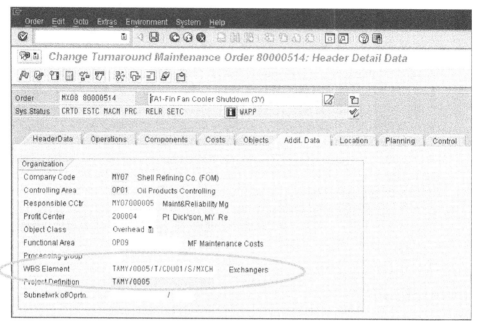

*Figure 4.2: TA work order assignment to WBS*

To ensure proper accounting treatment each TA work order has to contain a settlement rule which allocates the actuals to the PPE section within the B/S. This entry is shown in Figure 4.3.

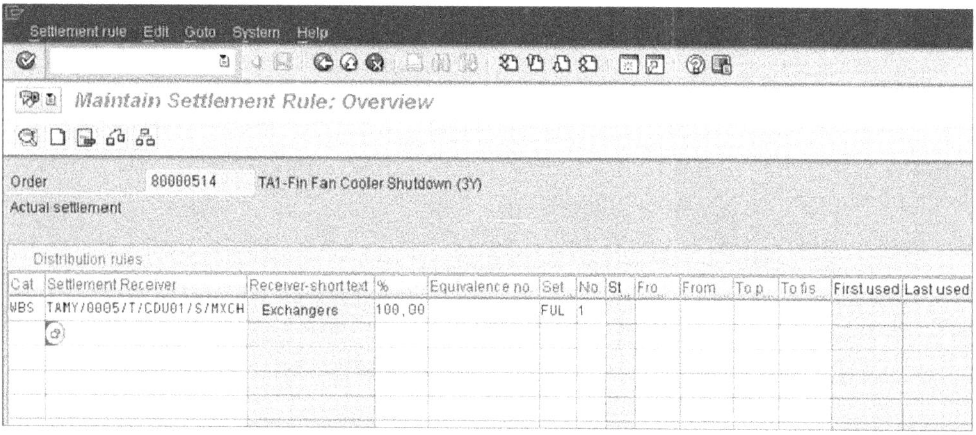

*Figure 4.3: TA work order settlement rule*

## 4.5 GAME – Statistical project (MX07) process

I would also like to introduce statistical projects, which require a certain type of work order – MX07 orders. Statistical projects are used for internal cost allocation purposes. In this context it is important to know that MX07 work orders only settle costs to cost centers, not to WBS elements! The main reason for this kind of project is the creation of transparency within internal process flows in order to track and proof their operating efficiency. The process flow for statistical projects is shown in Figure 4.4 below.

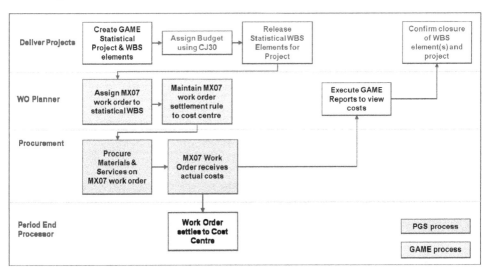

*Figure 4.4: Statistical project process*

## 4.6 MX07 work order – assignment to WBS

As I noted in section 4.4 TA work order – assignment to WBS" with regard to MX06 and MX08 work orders, MX 07 work orders also have to be linked to a WBS element and must contain a settlement rule. This is illustrated in Figure 4.5 and Figure 4.6.

75

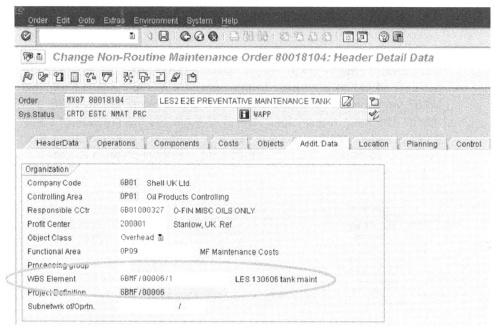

Figure 4.5: MX07 assignment to WBS

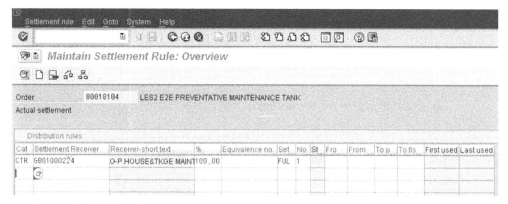

Figure 4.6: MX07 settlement rule

## 4.7    Direct asset purchase process

This section looks at another kind of special projects, the direct asset purchase. This process is relevant for tangible assets, for example a new company car or office furniture. The actuals are settled immediately after the GR is posted. The underlying process is illustrated in Figure 4.7. This type of projects contains only WBS elements but no network activities! The main purpose of using a project for the direct asset purchase process is the ability to use the governance process.

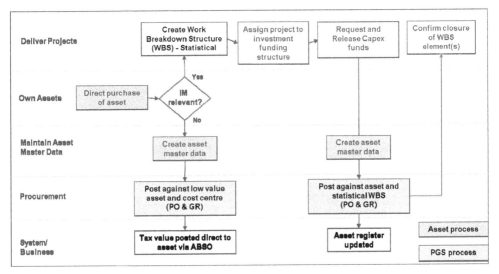

*Figure 4.7: Direct asset purchase process*

## 4.8 Investment/ goodwill asset process

The next section will cover the investment, or asset process. Although this is not main topic of my book I would nevertheless like show the process flow for this topic, which can be a key part of the merger & acquisition arena in Figure 4.8.

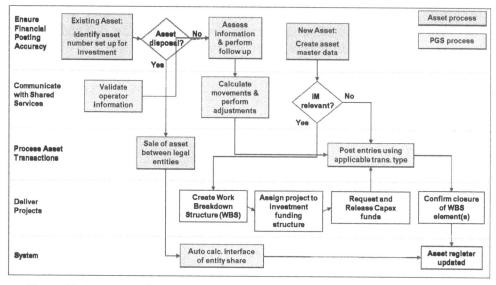

*Figure 4.8: Investment/Goodwill asset process*

## 4.9 Joint Venture projects

JV projects are the most frequent form of investments within the oil and gas industry. Commonly they are comprised of two equal partners (50:50 shares) for a certain term of service. One of these partners takes the lead role and has a major influence on financial processes. Usually one partner takes the lead for all administrative services, which includes the set-up and controlling of the project within the SAP system. So JV's can either be entity led or third party managed as illustrated in Figure 4.9.

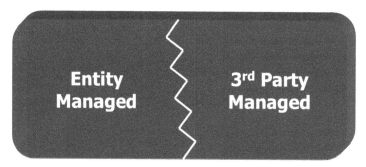

*Figure 4.9: Most frequent joint venture setup*

## 4.10  JV project profile – 3rd party managed

A JV project design has a major impact on the SAP system. For example, if the design is 50:50 with regard to funding, the appropriated funds must be traceable within SAP as well. Figure 4.10 shows the entry screen for a third party managed project profile. The project type has to be a development project.

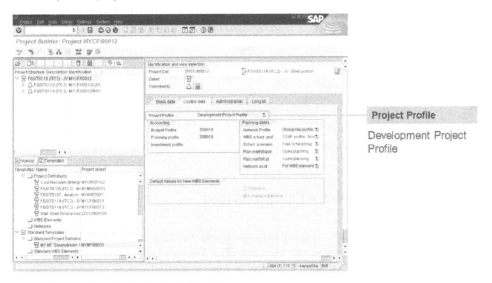

*Figure 4.10: JV project profile 3rd party*

## 4.11  JV project process – 3rd party managed

Figure 4.11 explains the JV project process for a third party managed project. It is worth noting that there might be non-recoverable costs, such as internal consulting services that are one-off costs with no return on investment. Separate WBS elements have to be setup and declared as cost elements which are able to receive and allocate costs.

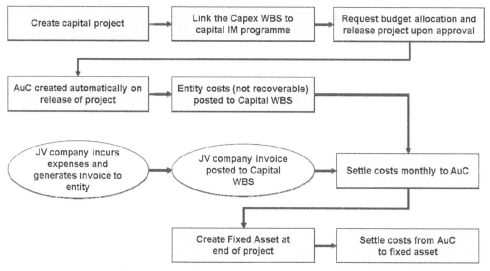

*Figure 4.11: JV project process 3rd party*

## 4.12 JV project profile – Entity managed

In the case that we are dealing with an entity managed JV project, the setup within SAP is a little bit different. The project type should be entered as a JV project, as demonstrated in Figure 4.12.

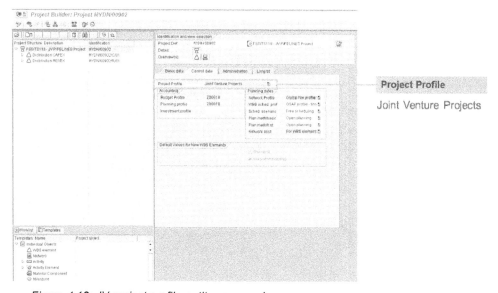

*Figure 4.12: JV project profile entity managed*

## 4.13  JV project process – Entity managed

Figure 4.13 shows the entity managed version of the JV project process. What is noteworthy in this context is the split between recoverable and non recoverable costs as shown in the different elements.

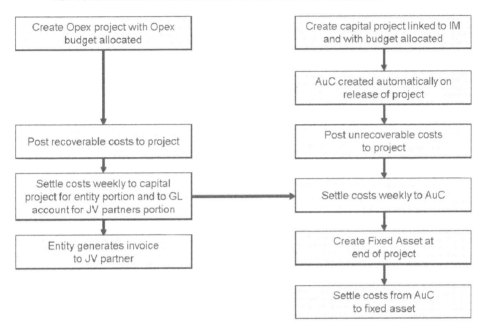

*Figure 4.13: JV project process entity managed*

## 4.14  Abandoned projects

Before wrapping up this section, I would like to review the last possible case: project abandonment. In SAP-PS and controlling terms there are four situations that are important to mention here:

- ▶ Abandoned projects containing (see also Figure 4.14):
- ▶ Costs on REVEX WBS
- ▶ Costs on CAPEX WBS and
- ▶ Costs already settled to fixed asset

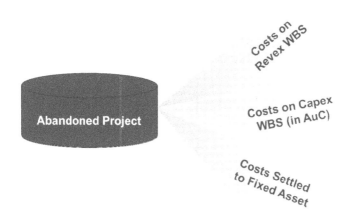

*Figure 4.14: Abandoned project costs*

Figure 4.15 deals with costs already settled on REVEX WBS. After the abandonment is agreed upon, all remaining costs on the project need to be settled to a final receiver, e.g. a cost center. The settlement rule for the REVEX WBS elements must be updated to reflect the cost center receiving the remaining costs.

**Costs on Revex WBS**

- All remaining costs on the project need to be settled to a final receiver.
- Revex WBS elements - settlement rule to be updated to reflect cost centre to receive remaining costs.

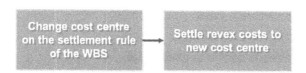

*Figure 4.15: Costs on REVEX WBS*

Figure 4.16 highlights the next possible option: costs on CAPEX WBS. All remaining costs on the projects needed to be settled to a final receiver. The settlement rule for the CAPEX WBS elements must be updated to reflect a cost center with a final settlement rule. The status of this element has to be changed to FUL (final settlement rule). All CAPEX costs in AuC will be settled to the cost center upon settlement. After that, the AuC balance will be automatically cleared out during the next settlement run.

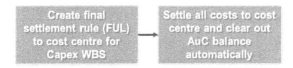

Costs on
Capex
WBS

- All remaining costs on the project need to be settled to a final receiver
- Capex WBS elements - settlement rule to be updated to reflect cost centre with a final settlement rule (FUL)
- All Capex costs in AuC will automatically be settled from the AuC to the cost centre upon settlement

Create final settlement rule (FUL) to cost centre for Capex WBS → Settle all costs to cost centre and clear out AuC balance automatically

*Figure 4.16: Costs on CAPEX WBS*

In some cases, there may already be costs settled to fixed assets (Figure 4.17). If the costs were partially capitalized at the time the project was abandoned they will occur in the asset register. If it is deemed that there is no economic value and further use to the company, these assets will need to be retired. The project manager must inform the asset owner to initiate the relevant process for asset retirement. After that, the asset costs are written-off against the final receiver (cost center).

**Costs Settled to Fixed Asset**

- Costs which have been partially capitalised at the time of the project abandonment will exist in the Asset Register

- If deemed to have no economic value and use to the company, these assets will need to be retired

- Project manager will inform *Own Assets* to initiate the asset process for Perform Retirement of Assets.

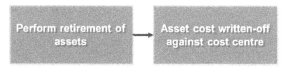

Perform retirement of assets ⟶ Asset cost written-off against cost centre

*Figure 4.17: Costs settled to fixed assets*

# 5 Project Reporting

In this chapter we'll explore controller's bread and butter — reporting.

## 5.1 SAP R/3 project reports

First, let's look at existing SAP R/3 and the relevant transaction codes:

- ▶ CJI3 – Display Project Actual Cost Line Items
- ▶ CJI5 – Display Project Commitment Line Items
- ▶ CJI8 – Display Project Budget Line Items
- ▶ S_ALR_87013534 – Plan 1/Plan 2/ Actual/Commitments
- ▶ ME5A – List Display of Purchase Requisitions
- ▶ ME2K – Purchasing Documents per Account Assignment
- ▶ /DS1/FI_C_PROJCOST – Project OC-1 Costing Report

In my experience, the most useful transaction codes are the first two on this list: CJI3 and CJI5. These transaction codes contain the most important information and contain both financial and commercial (contracting and procurement) data. As I have mentioned previously, the commercial data is essential for tracking the commitments through all project phases. The status of the existing purchase requisitions and purchase orders is viable with transaction CJI5. This report contains the status/deletion flag, the order limit, etc.

## 5.2 OC1-Sheet

The most frequent report within project controlling in the oil and gas industry is the OC1-sheet. OC1 is an abbreviation for overall costs, which covers the requirement to state and present all costs related to the project.

Let's first look at the available selection parameters in the entry screen, illustrated in Figure 5.1.

▶ Project parameters: one or more project definitions can be entered in cases where an individual is responsible not only for a single project, but for a project portfolio.

▶ Report display: the display of the OC1 sheet can occur either in hierarchical form or as a flat report. This is shown in Figure 5.2 and Figure 5.3.

▶ Defaults: this option contains the selected range of G/L accounts, for example.

▶ Budget: there is the option to display either the overall budget or the annually phased figures.

▶ Currency: enables you to generate the report either in local currency, e.g. Euro or in controlling currency, e.g. US-Dollar.

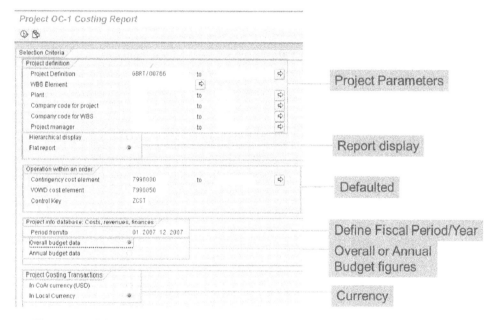

*Figure 5.1: OC1 selection parameters*

Figure 5.2 shows the OC1 report as a flat list. As this variant is not very clearly laid out, I prefer to use the hierarchical display which allows you to perform an in depth analysis via a drill down application. The figure also shows the maximum of the available columns in the report.

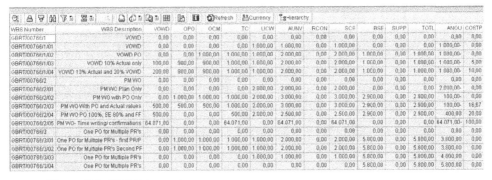

| WBS Number | WBS Description | VOWD | OPO | OCM | TC | UCW | AUNV | RCON | SCE | BSE | SUPP | TOTL | ANOU | COSTP |
|---|---|---|---|---|---|---|---|---|---|---|---|---|---|---|
| GBRT/00766/1 | VOWD | 0,00 | 0,00 | 0,00 | 0,00 | 0,00 | 0,00 | 0,00 | 0,00 | 0,00 | 0,00 | 0,00 | 0,00 | 0,00 |
| GBRT/00766/1/01 | VOWD | 0,00 | 0,00 | 0,00 | 0,00 | 1.000,00 | 1.000,00 | 0,00 | 1.000,00 | 0,00 | 0,00 | 0,00 | 1.000,00- | 0,00 |
| GBRT/00766/1/02 | VOWD PO | 0,00 | 0,00 | 1.000,00 | 1.000,00 | 1.000,00 | 2.000,00 | 0,00 | 2.000,00 | 1.000,00 | 0,00 | 1.000,00 | 1.000,00- | 0,00 |
| GBRT/00766/1/03 | VOWD 10% Actual only | 100,00 | 900,00 | 900,00 | 1.000,00 | 1.000,00 | 2.000,00 | 0,00 | 2.000,00 | 1.000,00 | 0,00 | 1.000,00 | 1.000,00- | 5,00 |
| GBRT/00766/1/04 | VOWD 10% Actual and 20% VOWD | 200,00 | 900,00 | 900,00 | 1.000,00 | 1.000,00 | 2.000,00 | 0,00 | 2.000,00 | 1.000,00 | 0,00 | 1.000,00 | 1.000,00- | 10,00 |
| GBRT/00766/2 | PM WO | 0,00 | 0,00 | 0,00 | 0,00 | 0,00 | 0,00 | 0,00 | 0,00 | 0,00 | 0,00 | 0,00 | 0,00 | 0,00 |
| GBRT/00766/2/01 | PM WO Plan Only | 0,00 | 0,00 | 0,00 | 0,00 | 2.000,00 | 2.000,00 | 0,00 | 2.000,00 | 0,00 | 0,00 | 0,00 | 2.000,00- | 0,00 |
| GBRT/00766/2/02 | PM WO with PO Only | 0,00 | 1.000,00 | 1.000,00 | 1.000,00 | 2.000,00 | 3.000,00 | 0,00 | 3.000,00 | 2.900,00 | 0,00 | 2.900,00 | 100,00- | 0,00 |
| GBRT/00766/2/03 | PM WO With PO and Actual values | 500,00 | 500,00 | 500,00 | 1.000,00 | 2.000,00 | 3.000,00 | 0,00 | 3.000,00 | 2.900,00 | 0,00 | 2.900,00 | 100,00- | 16,67 |
| GBRT/00766/2/04 | PM WO PO 100%, SE 90% and FF | 500,00 | 0,00 | 0,00 | 500,00 | 2.000,00 | 2.500,00 | 0,00 | 2.500,00 | 2.900,00 | 0,00 | 2.900,00 | 400,00 | 20,00 |
| GBRT/00766/2/05 | PM WO- Time writing/ confirmations | 64.071,00 | 0,00 | 0,00 | 64.071,00 | 0,00 | 64.071,00 | 0,00 | 64.071,00 | 0,00 | 0,00 | 0,00 | 64.071,00- | 100,00 |
| GBRT/00766/3 | One PO for Multiple PR's | 0,00 | 0,00 | 0,00 | 0,00 | 0,00 | 0,00 | 0,00 | 0,00 | 0,00 | 0,00 | 0,00 | 0,00 | 0,00 |
| GBRT/00766/3/01 | One PO for Multiple PR's - first PR/P | 0,00 | 1.000,00 | 1.000,00 | 1.000,00 | 1.000,00 | 2.000,00 | 0,00 | 2.000,00 | 5.800,00 | 0,00 | 5.800,00 | 3.800,00 | 0,00 |
| GBRT/00766/3/02 | One PO for Multiple PR's Second PF | 0,00 | 1.000,00 | 1.000,00 | 1.000,00 | 1.000,00 | 2.000,00 | 0,00 | 2.000,00 | 5.800,00 | 0,00 | 5.800,00 | 3.800,00 | 0,00 |
| GBRT/00766/3/03 | One PO for Multiple PR's | 0,00 | 0,00 | 0,00 | 0,00 | 1.000,00 | 1.000,00 | 0,00 | 1.000,00 | 5.800,00 | 0,00 | 5.800,00 | 4.800,00 | 0,00 |
| GBRT/00766/3/04 | One PO for Multiple PR's | 0,00 | 0,00 | 0,00 | 0,00 | 0,00 | 0,00 | 0,00 | 0,00 | 5.800,00 | 0,00 | 5.800,00 | 5.800,00 | 0,00 |

*Figure 5.2: OC1 flat report*

In Figure 5.3, I give you a hint about what I like about the OC1 report display mode. It is the hierarchical format, which also allows you to expand the existing WBS structure of the project. Moreover, I want to explain a bit more about the most crucial columns and their subject matter.

VOWD: value of work done, comprising of the actuals of goods received and invoices received plus the monthly posted VOWD accruals and time writing or own labor. VOWD is the most important KPI used to track the progress of the project. VOWD accruals are posted for goods and services already received, but not yet invoiced. When the invoices are processed, the accruals are reversed automatically. VOWD is posted on the level of each single purchase order, so it is crucial to implement financial controls in the early stages in order to ensure a proper progress monitoring.

- ▶ OPO (outstanding purchase orders): outstanding commitments on purchase orders.
- ▶ OCM (outstanding commitments): committed goods and services not yet received.
- ▶ UCW (uncommitted work): value of work still to be committed.
- ▶ TC (total commitments): includes as well purchase requisitions and purchase orders.
- ▶ AUNV (anticipated ultimate net value of work): TC + UCW
- ▶ RCON (required contingency): general contingency costs.
- ▶ SCE (site current estimate): best estimate of the final cost (AUNV+RCON)
- ▶ BSE (base estimate): original budget

87

▶ SUPP: supplementary and returned budget. In the event an overspend is foreseeable, the project has to initiate a supplementary investment proposal.

▶ TOTL: total budget (BSE+SUPP).

▶ ANOU (anticipated over/under spend): difference between total budget and total project costs.

▶ COSTP (cost progress): actual costs as a percentage of AUNV

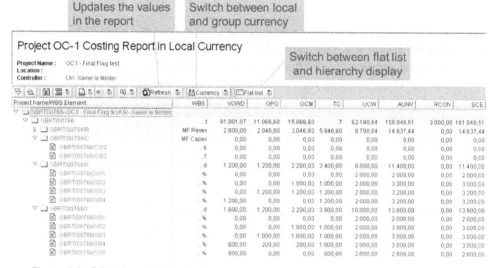

*Figure 5.3: OC1 hierarchical display*

The hierarchical display includes a refresh option in order to view the real time expenditures. It might also be relevant to switch between the local currency and the controlling currency, especially if the project is executed in a different currency then the controlling currency, e.g. EURO versus US-Dollar.

Last but not least, the report can be switched back into the flat format.

# 6 Wrap-up and conclusion

**After covering this content, I would like to leave you with a few recommendations not only on SAP topics, but also on my personal experiences in the project arena.**

One overall piece of advice I can clearly state as the beginning of this chapter is not to underestimate the **handling of all stakeholders**. From authorities and neighbors, to politicians and the board; it is crucial to set up a register of all relevant stakeholders and assign accountable individuals who communicate with them on a regular basis.

Set up WBS as early as possible:

Once the project scope is defined and frozen, and a high quality cost estimation is obtainable, the WBS's should be agreed upon and put into the system. Some materials and equipment have a long lead time with procurement periods of up to eighteen months. Having a WBS available early in the process enables suitable procurement and cost tracking from the very beginning of the project.

Track commitments especially during the execution and completion phases:

This seems to be an easy and obvious point, but I cannot stress enough that this topic deserves a tremendous amount of attention! Why is that? Every commitment shrinks the budget for the amount of the related purchase order, which means the budget is not available for other project items. If the budget is not made available in one large bucket, but in portions, long-term contracts should be split up in smaller portions until the final investment decision is granted. I emphasize this in particular for service orders. For example, an externally hired discipline engineer who is assigned to a multi-year contract can cause issues during planning and design phases if the final investment decision is delayed for whatever reason.

Assign budget and the relevant WBS elements to discipline engineers and make them responsible:

Similarly to my recommendation regarding setting up the WBS's early, on large projects it is very helpful to split up the budget, define sub-projects, and assign the associated budget and WBS elements to sub-project leads. The WBS acts as an account code and enables the procurement processes, as well as a proper asset accounting when the asset is finished. One follow up action of every project is a benchmarking exercise tracking the spend on staffing, equipment, and claims. So projects can be made comparable, thus every project has its own features.

Assign the contingency budget only to the project manager and track the changes in a separate change log:

I also recommend that you track scope changes that result in payments if unavoidable. Otherwise stick to a strict no change policy during project execution.

Assign budget to the construction manager and to the HSSE manager in order to avoid hiccups:

I have faced tremendous challenges during execution and completion phases, because there was no budget assigned to the aforementioned disciplines. As these are the two key players in finishing a project, they must be held accountable for their aspects of the budget as well.

Assign the PFM role as part of the project management team, keeping a straight line into the local finance organization, but with an additional straight line to the project manager:

In traditionally organized projects, the project manager wants to spend as little time with non-engineering disciplines as possible, so the classic project organization contains one project service manager who is in charge of all service related project functions like contracting and procurement, finance, cost estimation, scheduling and nowadays risk management. From my perspective, the finance function should be kept independent so the controller can act as last point of call if required.

Link the risk register for the project to the relevant WBS elements in order to show the value/costs of each risk included in the register:

Risk management might be the most unpopular aspect of the project business, but I think if it is possible to combine the project structure in SAP with the risk register, it is crucial to show the monetary value of the potential risks. Projects usually require a special insurance policy, so this can be extremely helpful to calculate the insurance disbursements.

Implement a RACI-matrix with job descriptions for all project jobs mentioned in this matrix to keep everyone not only accountable, but also responsible:

I recommend finishing the project execution plan in line with the organizational chart and job descriptions, as the lack of these documents offers easy findings for each review/audit carried out during the project. In my experience, a multi-week visit from any audit function can hamper the progress of the project.

Establish SAP as the one and only commonly agreed source for reporting purposes:

This is the only way to avoid the very popular MS Excel graveyards. I have struggled a lot on this front, but it is worth the effort. There should be only one system that everyone on the project uses. In other words, SAP should be agreed upon as the only acceptable source of figures included in the reporting. There should be no other system like MS Excel in order to bypass SAP.

Last but not least make SAP focal point and provide training to all key users within the project:

Usually all non-administrative functions are not used to working with SAP on a regular basis, for controllers it is. So I encourage every project controller to establish a strong reputation as a go-to person in providing this service for the project team and especially for the project management. Aside from technical skills, project controlling as a project management function relies a lot on communication and soft skills. Moreover visibility, i.e. not only at management meetings, but also at the construction site, are key elements of establishing trustworthy relationships amongst the project team and the stakeholders, e.g. local authorities, neighbors and environmental organizations.

## You have finished the book.

# A  The Author

**Michael Esser** currently serves as a Project Controller at Shell Deutsch-land Oil GmbH, Cologne. He is responsible for all accounting, control-ling, and economics and all other commercial topics related to major investment projects. Michael serves as interface between the project management team and the site leadership team. Prior to his current role, Michael held several key lead auditor and asset accounting roles at KPMG, Lekkerland & Tobaccoland, and Warth & Klein Grant Thornton. He holds a Master of Business Administration from the University of Co-logne.

# B   Definition of Terms & Acronyms

I have used the following terms in this e-book:

**Investment program** – data object that provides budgeting and approval processes over a discrete collection of cost objects representing potential initiatives

**Investment program definition** – clustered by class of business or line of business, e.g., Retail, B2B, etc.

**Investment program position** – node in the overall investment program and the investment management hierarchy structure is built using this position.

**Approval year** indicates that costs were approved this year, but not necessarily for expenditure in this year

**Person responsible** – person identified in the Manual of Authorities as having discretionary control over expenditure at that level

**Investment measures** are WBS elements, maintenance Orders or Internal Orders linked to Investment Positions

**Work Breakdown Structure** – hierarchical view of a project

**Network** – a process oriented view of the project

**Network Activities** – classified into internal, external, service and general cost activities including contingency

Commonly Used Acronyms:

AI – Asset integrity

AUC – Asset under construction

B/S – Balance sheet

CAPEX – Capital expenditure

CoB – Class of business

ERP – Enterprise resource planning

FID – Final investment decision

FMC – Facilities management companies

GAAP – Generally accepted accounting practice

GAME – Global asset management excellence

GR – Goods receipt

HSE – Health, safety and environment

HSSE – Health safety security and environment

IFRS – International financial reporting standards

IM – Investment management

IP – Investment proposal

IR – Invoice receipt

iPMS – Integrated Project Management System

JV – Joint venture

LE – Latest estimate

LoB – Line of business

MAPS – Methodology for process standardization

MF – Manufacturing

MoA – Manual of authority

NPV – Net present value

OIP – Operational implementation plan

OP – Oil products

OPEX – Operating expenditure

OPR – Opportunity realization process

PCR – Post completion review, Project change request

PEP – Project execution plan

PIR – Post implementation review

PIP – Project implementation plan

P/L – Profit and loss account

PMM – Project management methodology

PO – Purchase order

PR – Purchase request

PS – Project systems

RACI – Responsible accountable consult inform matrix

REVEX – Revenue expenditure

SBC – Sell to business customer

SCM – Supply chain management

SD – Sustainable development

SEM – Strategic enterprise management

SME – Subject matter expert

SOW – Statement of work

SRC – Sell to retail customer

T&R – Targets & Resources

ToR – Terms of reference

VIR – Value investment ratio

VOWD – Value of work done

WBS – Work breakdown structure

WIP – Work in progress

# C Disclaimer

This publication contains references to the products of SAP SE.

SAP, R/3, SAP NetWeaver, Duet, PartnerEdge, ByDesign, SAP BusinessObjects Explorer, StreamWork, and other SAP products and services mentioned herein as well as their respective logos are trademarks or registered trademarks of SAP SE in Germany and other countries.

Business Objects and the Business Objects logo, BusinessObjects, Crystal Reports, Crystal Decisions, Web Intelligence, Xcelsius, and other Business Objects products and services mentioned herein as well as their respective logos are trademarks or registered trademarks of Business Objects Software Ltd. Business Objects is an SAP company.

Sybase and Adaptive Server, iAnywhere, Sybase 365, SQL Anywhere, and other Sybase products and services mentioned herein as well as their respective logos are trademarks or registered trademarks of Sybase, Inc. Sybase is an SAP company.

SAP SE is neither the author nor the publisher of this publication and is not responsible for its content. SAP Group shall not be liable for errors or omissions with respect to the materials. The only warranties for SAP Group products and services are those that are set forth in the express warranty statements accompanying such products and services, if any. Nothing herein should be construed as constituting an additional warranty.

# More Espresso Tutorials Books

Martin Munzel:

## New SAP® Controlling Planning Interface

► Introduction to Netweaver Business Client

► Flexible Planning Layouts

► Plan Data Upload from Excel

*http://5011.espresso-tutorials.com*

Dieter Schlagenhauf & Jörg Siebert:

## SAP® Fixed Assets Accounting (FI-AA)

► Processes and Functions in SAP ERP Financials

► Validation and Reporting for IFRS

► Posting Examples

► Periodic Activities Explained

*http://5023.espresso-tutorials.com*

Anurag Barua:

## First Steps in SAP® Crystal Reports

► Basic end-user navigation

► Creating a basic report from scratch

► Formatting to meet individual presentation needs

*http://5017.espresso-tutorials.com*

Stefan Eifler:

# Quick Guide to SAP® CO-PA (Profitability Analysis)

- ▶ Basic organizational entities and master data
- ▶ Define the actual value flow
- ▶ Set up a planning environment
- ▶ Create your own reports

*http://5018.espresso-tutorials.com*

Kermit Bravo & Scott Cairncross:

# SAP® Enterprise Performance Management (EPM) Add-In

- ▶ Learn about the Connection Concept
- ▶ Get familiar with the SAP EPM Add-In for Excel and BPC 10.1
- ▶ Create a Basic Report from Scratch
- ▶ Walk through a Detailed Case Study

*http://5042.espresso-tutorials.com*

Tanya Duncan:

# Practical Guide to SAP® CO-PC (Product Cost Controlling)

- ▶ Cost Center Planning Process and Costing Run Execution
- ▶ Actual Cost Analysis & Reporting
- ▶ Controlling Master Data
- ▶ Month End Processes in Details

*http://5064.espresso-tutorials.com*

Ann Cacciottolli:

# First Steps in SAP® Financial Accounting (FI)

- ▶ Overview of key SAP Financials functionality and SAP ERP integration
- ▶ Step-by-step guide to entering transactions
- ▶ SAP Financials reporting capabilities
- ▶ Hands-on instruction based on examples and screenshots

*http://5095.espresso-tutorials.com*

www.ingramcontent.com/pod-product-compliance
Lightning Source LLC
Chambersburg PA
CBHW070846070326
40690CB00009B/1725